ATLAS POETICA
A Journal of World Tanka

Number 40

M. Kei, editor
Grunge, editorial assistant
Kira Nash, technical assistant

Summer, 2020
Keibooks, Perryville, Maryland, USA

KEIBOOKS

P O Box 346
Perryville, Maryland, USA 21903
AtlasPoetica.org / Twitter: Keibooks1

Atlas Poetica
A Journal of World Tanka

Copyright © 2020 by Keibooks

All rights reserved. No part of this book may be reproduced in any form or by any electronic or mechanical means including information storage and retrieval systems without permission in writing from the publisher, except by reviewers and scholars who may quote brief passages. See our EDUCATIONAL USE NOTICE.

Atlas Poetica : A Journal of World Tanka, an organic print and e-journal published at least three times a year. *Atlas Poetica* is dedicated to publishing and promoting world tanka literature, including tanka, kyoka, gogyoshi, tanka prose, tanka sequences, shaped tanka, sedoka, mondo, cherita, zuihitsu, ryuka, and other variations and innovations in the field of tanka. We do not publish haiku, except as incidental to a tanka collage or other mixed-form work.

Atlas Poetica is interested in all verse of high quality, but our preference is for tanka literature that is authentic to the environment and experience of the poet. While we will consider tanka in the classical Japanese style, our preference is for fresh, forward-looking tanka that engages with the world as it is. We are willing to consider experiments and explorations as well as traditional approaches.

In addition to verse, *Atlas Poetica* publishes articles, essays, reviews, interviews, letters to the editor, etc., related to tanka literature. Tanka in translation from around the world are welcome in the journal.

Published by Keibooks

Print ISBN-13: 979-8648894426

Available in print and ebook.

AtlasPoetica.org

TABLE OF CONTENTS

Editorial
Special Tanka Translation Project, M. Kei 5
Educational Use Notice 92
Editorial Biographies 92

Poetry
A. A. Marcoff 7, 8
ai li 10, 11, 12, 13
Alexander Alyapkin / Александр Аляпкин 14
Alexis Rotella 15
Amelia Fielden 19, 86
Andrew M. Bowen 20
an'ya 84
Autumn Noelle Hall 21
Bruce England 22
Bryan Rickert 23
Carol Raisfeld 24, 25, 26, 28
Carole Johnston 28, 29
Chen-ou Liu 30
Chris Bullard 31
Cullen Whisenhunt 31
Dave Read 31, 32
Debbie Strange 33
Elisa Theriana 33
Elizabeth Howard 34, 35
Fractled 36
Gabriel Martins 37
Gail Brooks 38
Genie Nakano 38
Geoffrey Winch 41
Gerry Jacobson 39, 40
Grunge 41
Hema Ravi 42
Hemapriya Chellappan 42
Ignatius Fay 43, 44, 45
Ingrid Kunschke 83, 84
Jackie Chou 46
James Tipton 84
Jan Foster 19
Jason Morgan 46
Joanna Ashwell 47
Johannes S. H. Bjerg 85
John Zheng 48
Joshua Michael Stewart 48, 49, 50
Joy McCall 14, 50, 51, 52, 58
Kala Ramesh 85
Karen O'Leary 53
Karla Linn Merrifield 54
Kath Abela Wilson 55, 87
Keitha Keyes 56
Kira Nash 57
Larry Kimmel 87
Liam Wilkinson 58
Lorne Henry 58
M. Kei 5, 41, 59, 82, 85
Margaret Knapke 52
Mark Jun Poulos 59, 60, 61
Marshall Bood 61
Matsukaze 62, 64
Mel Goldberg 85
Michael H. Lester 65, 66, 67, 68, 69
Michael McClintock 85
Michael O'Brien 69
N. Nyberg 70
Nathalie Lauro 71
Neal Whitman 72
Patricia Prime 73
Paul Callus 53
Paul Smith 86
Random Poetry Generator 41
Raquel D. Bailey 86
Ray Spitzenberger 74
Roary Williams 86
Rp Verlaine 74
Saeko Ogi 86
Sandra Renew 75
Sanford Goldstein 86
Scott Moss 75
Sterling Warner 76
Tanja Trček 77
Taofeek Ayeyemi/ Táófíkì Ayéyemí 78
Tim Gardener 79
Tim Lenton 80
Yasaman Etemadi 81
William Altoft 81
Zane Parks 81

Articles
Tanka Translation Project, M. Kei 82
Review: *Light-Borne Rain*, by Shelia Windsor & Larry Kimmel, reviewed by Patricia Prime 88

Announcements 89

Special Tanka Translation Project

Atlas Poetica is an international journal of tanka and related literature. In our forty issues over more than ten years, we have published tanka in thirty-seven languages with translation appearing in all but five issues. With this issue, we invite you to join us in extending tanka translation more broadly still. With the permission and cooperation of more than a dozen tanka poets and translators, we are inaugurating a special Tanka Translation Project to run in this issue and the next.

The guidelines for participating in the Tanka Translation Project and a sample collection are provided in this issue. More than a dozen tanka poets whose work has appeared in the pages of *Take Five : Best Contemporary Tanka* have granted permission for their works to be translated in non-profit and educational venues without needing to seek their individual permission. Anyone and everyone is invited to try their hand at translation by translating any or all of these specially selected tanka to any language of which they have knowledge. Translations will be printed on a space available basis in ATPO 41, Autumn, 2020. Those published translations will become part of the Tanka Translation Project. Your submission of a translation for the projection with the subject line of 'Tanka Translation Project' indicates your acceptance of the rules for the project. For more details, see the article.

Atlas Poetica provides bylines and biographies for all translators, including when the poet is the translator. To be a translator is an extraordinarily difficult job; a translator must not only be skilled in two languages, they must be a poet as well. It is translators who first made Japanese tanka available in English and other languages, and who continue to expand our access to Japanese tanka and scholarship. As a living poetry that has been continuously published for fourteen hundred years, it would take an army of translators to make it all available to readers around the world.

In addition, tanka is composed in many other languages, English in particular, but also French, Romanian, and other European languages. Tanka continues to expand into other languages as a truly international body of literature. Tanka poets of India and other South Asian countries at home and in Diaspora are numerous. Tanka has reached Africa and now appears in various languages in Western Africa, such as Fante and Twi, but also appearing intermittently in other languages of the continent. Thanks to its small size, tanka is a portable poetry. Its emphasis on image and its trust in the reader means that tanka can be read by people of many different backgrounds. The words of the poet unite with the spirit of the reader to create a multitude of poems that appear like sunsets: each reader sees something a little different from everyone else, but all experience the same sun.

The past year has been particularly challenging for me as I have struggled with my health, then the effects of the global pandemic. For that reason, I skipped the spring issue of *Atlas Poetica*. Better late than never. ATPO operates on an organic schedule and has for several years as I have wrestled with finding a compromise between the work of the journal and managing my personal affairs in days of increasing health problems. For the same reason, I have had to cancel the planned online chapbook series originally announced for this year. I am concentrating on the core mission of producing the journal and website.

Special thanks to Michael H. Lester, Joy McCall, Debbie Strange, and Yvette Castille for their donations of support during the time of the covid-19 pandemic. It means a lot to have faithful supporters.

~K~

M. Kei
Editor, *Atlas Poetica*

Egypt's Lake Nasser was created by completion of the Aswan High Dam in 1970. Sunglint (light reflected off the water surface) on the lake makes it easily visible.
<http://earthobservatory.nasa.gov/Features/ISSArt/Images/14618_lrg.jpg>. *Cover image courtesy of Earth Observatory, NASA.*

echoes

A. A. Marcoff

a mountain, beautifully formed, within the conjunction of snow—the whole thing held in low mist or cloud—the snow like some eternity of white, of stillness, and the consubstantial aura of dawn: a red sun rises in the sky like Japan: leaves fall into a deep well: I stare into the well, the well of memory, of dreams: I remember how students at Tokyo University were once quizzed as to which novel had most influenced them in their lives: the clear winner was 'Crime and Punishment': and in second place came Natsume Soseki's 'Kokoro' (the heart)—which concerned matters of suicide and obligation in the Japanese way: how a man felt responsible for another man's suicide and, years later, takes the same path to regain his own honour: and I remember Shusaku Endo's 'Silence', a book about how trained Jesuit missionaries in late medieval Japan apostatised their faith when faced with cruelty and the systematic execution of their local converts by the samurai: that is, when faced with the silence of God in such a situation of horror, and darkness: and then there was 'Shogun': all about the Englishman shipwrecked in old Japan, who becomes very Japanese, and as I finished the book I did myself wonder if I would ever be able to leave Japan, and felt a sense of entrapment, deep in my bones: that country is the snowiest region on earth, and now I feel the snow falling gently in my dreams, gently falling on the ground in the Taishakuten Temple one winter in old Tokyo, when it was dark except for a lantern, the whole scene being immaculate with magic and seeming: near the entrance there was a ladle and some holy water to pour over the effigy of a man, so to wash away one's sins, to be pure, to be whole...

I visited the graves of 'The 47 Ronin' (masterless samurai): when their lord had to commit ritual suicide for a misdemeanour, those ronin took revenge on the man responsible, and then all 47 of them committed hara-kiri to atone: I watched an old lady, in full and best kimono, burn incense and pray for their spirits, for their pure samurai code of honour: sometimes I paid my respects to a small Shinto shrine near where I lived in Katsushika-ku, in north-east Tokyo: this shrine was dedicated to the god of the fox: I went through the torii or gateway, pulled the cord to ring the bell and awaken the god inside, and stood back and clapped my hands together, making my prayer, and then bowing...

sometimes at night I went to a local river, an extensive river that existed behind all the roadways and labyrinths of paths and alleyways and all the conurbation or wasteland in the area: and the river swept my worries and problems into the moon, which illuminated my mind with its haunting light and benediction, accepting me into its grace of moments within the passage of eternal time: and there were art exhibitions in department stores where well-dressed attendants welcomed you into the lifts, bowing to you as you entered and departed: and I would walk by the Sumida River in Asakusa in the evening, and often approached the old Sensoji Temple by taking a path through an arcade which sold traditional Japanese umbrellas:

> my waxed orange & white
> Japanese umbrella—
> I carry beauty
> into
> rain

I went through an avenue of trees to the temple, in the dark, all lit up by Chinese paper lanterns in the colours of the world, and stood there, by a huge bronze brazier, where hundreds of incense sticks were burning: and I used my hand to waft incense smoke into my hair and face, to prepare and purify myself: so I climbed the stone steps to the dark wooden temple, said my prayer to Kannon, the goddess of compassion, or mercy, and became for these moments the passing of dreams over deep Japanese ground...

and I remember visiting my friend Mr Kudo, a teacher of English in Kashima, near the sea east of Tokyo: he had studied Russian at Tokyo University, and saw me with my Russian background as an opportunity to get close to Mother Russia: he did once take me to a Russian restaurant, where we drank a lot of vodka and got very drunk: but in Kashima he took me to see a famous shrine, where Basho had long ago written a great haiku: and it was gorgeous within: I asked him which he preferred, haiku or tanka, and he answered 'tanka', because 'tanka are more romantic': and on one occasion, after a big party there, we all got up hungover in the morning, and went for a walk in the nearby forest: and for me it was a nightmare — so many shocks in Japan: our path through the trees was blocked by immense cobwebs, inhabited by big black spiders that wove their malice between branches: it was like the film 'Throne of Blood', where a Japanese Macbeth-figure meets the witches in Cobweb Forest: I had to duck beneath all this sinister resonance, this cobwebbing of a nightmare that stuck to my thoughts like evil . . .

and yet the land was pure Shinto, everything around you animated and energised by the sacred — where the wind or even the ground was vital and vibrant with spirit or god — where that rock could be your ancestor and the trees and rivers and the sun were enlivened by gods: and once, months later, I sat contemplating the Zen rock garden at the Ryoanji Temple in Kyoto, and learned how the Japanese value mysterious beauty (*yūgen*), and the unknowable, and the unanswerable, and I thought of Keats's theory of 'negative capability': these are the Zen graphics of the world — that a mountain could be sketched in a quick splash of ink — that a whole mountain range could be reflected in the eye of a dragonfly — that you could hold the wind in your hand like a butterfly . . .

and this rock garden could be sublime and enigmatic, just like the universe — and yet at the end of the day it might be just a few stones and some gravel, practical and ordinary again: and I think of all those I met in Japan, who taught me, and inspired my thoughts with beauty: and I recall all the characters I met, how they appeared long ago and then vanished: perhaps I'll meet them again, in some other world, of mists, and timings: I write:

>   people come & go
>   those I loved
>   those I lost
>   those I longed for
>   this world of light & shadow

even so these echoes, these ruins of light: and I went at last to the coast, and regarded the primordial sea, and all that long and stony shore — the shore of eternity — and contemplated the fading of day and the coming of twilight, and looked out over the sea in Japan — Japan the transformer — and the sky was rust: and finally I wrote:

>   of course
>   it will all end
>   in death
>   she sings late into the evening
>   watching the genius of waves

~*Leatherhead, in the Mole Valley, England*

a vision of spring

A. A. Marcoff

I sit in the old church like silence: outside in the open air, it is fresh and cool, a spring day, and when I fed the birds with multiple seeds, a dunnock came to me close as breath: there is distribution of open sun and shadow: here, in this old church, there are pillars of light on the stone floor: in this place I try to comprehend my existence: I contemplate the transeptal and conceptual, the glass stained with colour — the colour of ideas, depictions that seem illuminated as light descends as dawn to the stone: this is old light, old wood, and silence: meaning is located in wood and stone, glass cast in the colours of a prism . . .

Mary, Mother of God, is adored amongst women: I am aware of symbols within the layout of a stone reality: aware too of the labours of faith and the stations of eternity: I see figureheads and carvings in this house of dreams and scriptures — dreams and scriptures that encroach upon the soul: the sun, the mind, light up your versions of the world: I remember how old cathedrals in France resembled gigantic beetles, with their flying buttresses extended like limbs of grey: Moses came as flame there, and Elijah, and Isaiah: but the church here has the shape of a cross, and circles represent eternity: as I sit down, a structure of light appears like a vision that binds my reality — a structure of light — epiphany, or mystery — the transfiguration of time here and now . . .

the altar is oriented towards the rising sun, eastwards in the morning: I have a nostalgia, a harking back, for older times, when hermits sought for God in the wilderness, amidst locusts and desert, or in caves and on pillars and lodged within rock: when they lived on remote islands with the herring gulls and kittiwakes and the wild winds of the North Sea, or the Atlantic: that was before it all became ordered, categorised, catalogued, when grey men conducted councils in the over-arching institutions of complicated faith: then there were bibliographies of moonlight, and the coding of pure word, that gospel spark reduced from simple flame to logics and dialectics . . .

once it was that tough men lived in wild places where gospels came like waves and eternity crashed like the sea into their minds — oceans of ultimate reality — the sheer sea and vast echoes and wind on the waters: they lived the weather and the wild — their gospel hardship, exposure, experience: they had nowhere else on Earth to be — just to be there — out in the vastness and the wilderness with nothing but them and God, and the hard cold wild: and so here in this church, I feel called into the spring, called to leave this silence and to walk out into dust: I stand now under the rainbow of the world, the morning choral with birdsong the colour of the sun:

>   spring rain
>   falls
>   to the ground like a gospel
>   the land
>   beautiful and fresh and green

so I walk from those apsidal houses and their indices into a land of wild tongues and realism, where butterflies soar on clouds of fire, their wings flaming with the sun in the steep and floating aura of spring, in the colours and wings of iconography, this land and its horizons of blue myth and sky — a sky that sings on the wing of a robin redbreast as it comes in to rest on the grasses and pastures and meadows: these are my steps towards the sun, as I walk out into a song — the fervent sounds and flowering of this land and green and flora, where the wind smells like earth — the purifying flame of a mind ignited with the spirit of gospel and water and tongue and stone . . .

I walk out into the equinox, cathedral that is forest, tall with canopies of sky, where squirrels scamper with bushy tails and energy: I walk into a garden — perhaps that garden — where daffodil and tulip exist, and cowslip, and primrose and aubrietia, all the colours of the land with its soil connecting the present with time eternal, the arrival of season as memory and latency, the impulse that harbours green abundance and bud, as swans build their nests on the river banks, the whole life-force and power that is spring immanent within the deep miracle and mystery of an egg — brilliant to the eye . . .

I walk by the river and follow it into spring — walk into its wild orthodoxy — its ecclesiastical robing and touch and currents — I read the dream of the world — I watch the flight of kingfishers that capture the light of the sun in their wings — the river reverenced and blue — moments that burn with the incense of time — in the twinkling of an eye and the force of silence — the arc of the sky itself like some great archway, with its aura of light amidst cloud — the sky white and grey and blue — into which the sun will rise:

> dawn is a fire
> in which
> I watch the river
> become
> the light of the waters of the world

this gloria celebrates — enfolds — all those apostles — who are walking in the contemplation of the white whiteness of lilies, the land planted with the gold of daffodil — that yellow silence of petals swaying in the breeze like prayer: in the circulation of seasons the blackthorn blossoms white with ambience by the course of this sweet river:

> spring again:
> years go by
> & still
> river and the blossom
> flow

spring — catharsis of leaf and willow and frond — the pink tinge of spring upon these trees — their buds packed with transmission: I follow the aisle of the river where the waters flow with light and sun and swan:

> a swan flies
> out of the dawn sky
> its wild white stream
> of
> existence

it is all white and pink with sky and blossom, in the living of the moment, and that gospel and its burning core charisma of Earth and mood and spirit, the sunlit wild cantata of reality . . .

~*Leatherhead, in the Mole Valley, England*

A A Marcoff — Tony is an Anglo-Russian poet, born in Iran, and has lived in Africa, France, Iran and Japan. He has been a university library assistant, a teacher, and has been in charge of poetry and creative writing in a large psychiatric hospital. A main-stream poet as well as a tanka poet, he has been widely published in journals such as 'Poetry Review'. He now lives near the beautiful River Mole.

tanka dark

ai li

the madhouse
i am quiet here
but i hear
someone singing
sakura

paper flowers
you will burn
these too
at
the same time

someone dancing
to an old rhythm
above me
i was 18 then
and she was alive

no one to wait up
for anymore
you intimated
your hair unwashed
your clothes stained

memories
you can't rely
on them anymore
undressing
in your front yard

this tanka life
even relationships
can be summed up
in
five lines

rain
i find myself
in a penny arcade
i must have stepped
through a portal

water plants
i try to name them
but the sound
of the stream
distracts me

in the morning sun
what i have to do
today is clear
i have to find myself
some happiness

~Singapore and London, UK

cherita perdu

ai li

weighed down with work
and money problems

he goes awol

finds feather boas
sequins and killer heels
his inner showgirl

your sari

caught
in the doorway

one
of the colours
of rajasthan

a fault line

under
your house

your excuse
for
his bad behaviour

woodland path

a ten year old
walking home
from school

becomes another
newspaper vanishing

looking back

raindrops
on the back windscreen

the farewell
already
a memory

my persian friend eating pistachios

into her night
her life of splendour

reduced to
stolen pleasures
in a distant land

choreographed
to ancient music

the dowager's
dream wanderings
into

cosmic space

a saffron sunset

the woman
on a rooftop

waving
in the last moments
of day

frogmen in the lake

a red sari
emerging from
the depths

a girl
barely fifteen

~Singapore and London, UK

riding tandem

ai li

rain watching
robin red
a little drier
under
a big leaf

i exchange

loneliness
for sex

when fall comes
and my cupboard's
bare

my bones
are younger
in these ruins
touched
by starlight

that day

remembering the ashes
of
burnt letters

love
that went astray

in
your roof garden
night has fallen
and so has
your stone cherub

the ritual

of lighting
candles

the ritual
of
going inside

one winter morning
the phone rang
and the speaker
was already
in black

standing up

for the national anthem
in the old cinema

an afternoon matinee
that only i
remember now

snacks
for the pow wow
the dead woman
defrosted them
before departing

~Singapore and London, UK

tanka solo

ai li

the lonely side
to travelling
faces unfamiliar
cold night rain
in used condoms

~Singapore and London, UK

cherita solo

ai li

she was shoplifting

from her wheelchair
a small bottle

of shampoo
our eyes met
hers were old

coming in

from the rain
to see
your face

after
the long distance call

~Singapore & London, UK

ai li is a Straits Chinese short form poet from London and Singapore who writes about Life, Love and Loss bringing healing and prayer to her poems. The creator of cherita, editor and publisher of the cherita, founding editor and publisher of still, moving into breath and dew-on-line, she is also an evidential spiritualist medium, an urban photographer, and a surrealist collage painter. Find her essence in the quiet of her inner rooms at: https://www.amazon.com/ai-li/e/B0080X6KOC/ref=sr_tc_2_0?qid=1469884842&sr=1-2-ent.

Belomorsky Woodworking Plant

Alexander Alyapkin & *Joy McCall*

our factory
is now completely destroyed.
150 years
from the date of onset
of the sawmill

 The history of the Woodworking Plant is tragic; family dynasties of working people worked on it.
 The workers worked 16 hours a day, their salaries were enough only for food, and they lived in wooden huts (in which many people still live today) in very poor houses.
 Many of them were women (they did heavy men's work)!
 The owners of the company lived well in London. The products of this company were shipped to the UK and other developed countries.
 The number of employees reached 1800 people. The plant was a city-forming enterprise, the center of the region's economy.
 In 2005, the enterprise ceased to exist, as did the whole city. I myself worked there. Most people moved far away.
 Only a few of us live here now, struggling for existence.

he lives day to day
in a wasteland now
thin and tired
still holding on
to home and hope

~Karelia, Russia / *Norwich, England*

Alexander Alyapkin lives a long distance from civilization in the north of the White Sea. He loves nature, and the forest around him. Karelia is located near Finland, we can say it is already Scandanavia! The winters are long and the summer is short. Alexander loves working with wood, and folk music. He makes flutes from fallen branches. (Etsy- Nord Wind Art)

Joy McCall lives in the small busy city of Norwich, England but she often wishes she lived in some wild distant forest with a great river running by.

risk / риск

Alexander Alyapkin

Alexander Alyapkin, Russian-English Translator

Александр Аляпкин, русско-английский переводчик

it is dangerous
for us to go
to the forest now
bears walk there
even around the city

это опасно место для нас
чтобы пойти в лес сейчас
медведи гуляют там
даже по всему городу

already three
mushroom pickers
have disappeared
in the woods
this year

уже трое
грибников
пропали
в лесу
этот году

~*Belomorsk, Karelia, Russia* / Беломорск, Карелия, Россия

Alexander Alyapkin lives a long distance from civilization in the north of the White Sea. He loves nature, and the forest around him. Karelia is located near Finland, we can say it is already Scandanavia! The winters are long and the summer is short. Alexander loves working with wood, and folk music. He makes flutes from fallen branches.

Александр Аляпкин живет очень далеко от цивилизации на севере Белого моря. Он любит природу и лес вокруг него. Карелия находится недалеко от Финляндии, можно сказать, это уже Скананавия! Зимы длинные, а лето короткое. Александр любит работать с деревом и народной музыкой. Он делает флейты из упавших веток.

Cherita

Alexis Rotella

Sorting through my portfolio

a pack of uneaten crackers
I took to drawing class

the tattooed contortionist
who posed for us
twelve years ago

~United States

Alexis Rotella

God said
I give you a starry night
now it's up to you
to connect
all the dots

A temple
where people stay
during metamorphosis
where foot rubs
are frequent and free

*Now that your malady
finally has a name
don't label it*
the healer
cautions

Long distance relationship
on the telephone
we gaze at
the same
autumn moon

The beautiful redhead
walks into
the party
suddenly the air
becomes prickly

A patient cancels
his appointment
because he's sick—
isn't that way
he should come?

A world of difference
between a Charles
and a Charlie
one of the things
I've learned in life

How many times
did we look at this house,
not once hearing
the kid next door
on trumpet?

*Pay attention to how
he treats his mother,*
Mom yells
as I run out the house
to a beeping horn

Walk at dusk
I meet a neighbor
who carries
a golf club
just in case

Haiku circle
the guy who stayed
in his room yesterday
first to arrive
in a new wheelchair

Nursing home
a woman talks about
her pet turtle
who climbed all the way
to the moon

Between bits of evening news
take this drug
the woman says smiling
*even though
it might kill you*

His last supper
blowfish
with some pretty
polka dot mushrooms
on the side

How can they do it
these women who walk around
exposing their breasts
my closet
filled with turtlenecks

Dinner party at the villa
on the hill
our American host
announces he has to pee
then returns in his birthday suit

Woman on welfare
she tells her little girl
one day
they'll have a house
filled with knick-knacks

I do us both
a favor—
letting him go
so he can find
someone else

Bags under the bags
under her eyes—
ghost of a woman
in a silver dress
early Kyoto morning

Cats waiting
on the hillside steps
the fisherman
throws them
his evening catch

Grandma works
in the Czarina's kitchen—
her bedroom
on the north side
absent of sun

The breakfast crumbs
my mother left on
her plate
I read them
like a poem

All her friends
have gotten so short
my mother says
she barely
five feet tall

So proud
of all the bruises
she collected
while staying with me—
my mother

In Venice—
searching for them
everywhere
the blinds for which
it is famous

By the creek
in the woods
he polishes his car
where tonight I won't
refuse his kiss

My mother
about to appear—
dear God,
the windows
need washing!

How they bother me,
my mother's quirks
yet how like
my mother
I am

New moon
over Palermo
the ice cream flavor—
of-the-day
squid ink

Not enough sun
for this old fig
but I keep it around
for the smell
of its leaves

No headstone
for the stillborn
named Rachel
buried at the bottom
of the hill

Almost ninety
my mother wants
to be
wherever
she's not

Always ready
to get up and go
my mother
who lives in
her coat

Man in the moon
he just sits there
looking down
at me
while eating gruel

She goes home
every weekend
my Slavic friend
whose mother
still bakes bread

The guy behind me
beeps his horn—
have another
double latte,
pal

September 11
not much to smile about
the land where
I picked mushrooms
now a burial ground

Triplets next door
play ball in a lightning storm—
nothing can touch them
they thought
until the sea took away their dad

The poet I emailed for years
refuses to speak to me
on the phone—
I wonder
if he stutters

Seminar break—
I speak with a woman
from Colorado . . .
everyone is lonely there
she sighs

Orange marigolds
they shiver
next to
the deep
purple sage

I deserve a man
who brings
me flowers
not a man
who thought of it

From the balcony above
a moonflower parachutes
its fragrance
into my lonely
loveless Saturday night

Come to think of it
I never met a Tom
who wasn't
a peck
of trouble

So tired
of my own whining
I throw
a book
at myself

Drugs drugs drugs,
is that all you know,
I scream
at the baby-faced doctor
who's just trying to help

No, he says,
I'm not a pedophile,
yet he lied
about almost
everything else

A dream come true—
the door of an ice cream truck
flies open
creamsicles and popsicles
lie at our feet

Cleaning lady
the skink sucked up
by the vacuum
as she continues
to hum

A patient says
she'll try
to drink more water—
there's that word again
"try"

Once he had a dog
the homeless man tells me—
holes in his red woolen gloves
as he caresses the ears
of our golden

Late summer
how some leaves
twirl down,
while others turn into
butterflies

After we feed each other fondue
and inhale each other's smoke
I say I'll slip
into something comfortable
and choose the back door

A taxi ride
through Central Park—
the fragrance
of magnolias
after last night's rape

~United States

Alexis Rotella is a visual storyteller well known for her digital art and photography as well as her many books of poetry, many of which are available on Kindle.

Perspectives

Amelia Fielden and *Jan Foster*

engagement photo
at Lake Yamanaka
the mountain
rising snow-streaked behind,
in the foreground just us

cool undertones
to your smiling comments
I search your eyes
 —it's dangerous
to love someone this much

fearlessly
my young grandson plunges
under the waves—
loving and letting go,
an eternal quandary

hanging baskets
a waterfall of blossoms
tumbling
around me, clouds of perfume
 . . . I'm free to dream

Je Reviens
always my favourite
French perfume
remembered by one lover
 . . . only by him

adrift on a raft
of social platitudes,
I detect
a whiff of ozone
ahead of the coming storm

swept away
by a 'southerly buster'
the suspicion
I should be somewhere else
doing something useful

clearing pathways
through the storm's debris,
it's alarming
how good at this
our family has become

surrounded
in old age by family,
not my karma—
though love can bridge distance
one plus none is still one

across the abyss
of loneliness, a lifeline
. . . this new friend
who shares my passion
for travelling

"better
to travel hopefully
than to arrive"—
hope is the blessing,
regard these late blooms

flights cancelled
long delays announced—
time
to rethink
the way ahead

~Australia

Amelia Fielden is a professional translator of Japanese literature, and a keen writer of Japanese form poetry in English. Her latest publication is 'These Purple Years', a life in tanka.

Jan Foster is a teacher of creative writing, whose favourite things include family, her garden, writing, a good book to read, and a cryptic crossword to conquer.

Andrew M. Bowen

Buttered steam rises
from pancake ponds tinged saffron
by sunrise, our first
in gray weeks of snow, almost
as cheery as Sarah's smile

Clouds and mist mate and
leach color from the twilight
as city lights birth
bars of white, green, blue, and gold
in puddles of melting snow

Copper-pipe hair, eyes
by Titian, and ski-slope curves
in tight red and black,
she moves like the queen of a
legend, and I'm the ogre

Three wild turkeys dart
across greening fields, little
tyrannosaurs in
search of food or mates, they give
hope Spring's finally arrived

Leaves skitter on my
roof like kittens scratching to
come in, but I think
it's just Jack Frost opening
the door for Old Man Winter

Pink and white blossoms
rustle beneath the gray sky
The west wind molds your
denim skirt against your thighs
and the day begins to warm

Iron beams and branches
materialize from the
twilight like gray ghosts
out to tour the city on
a day of murk and drizzle

The risen moon, a
half-eaten lemon crème pie,
beams down the railroad
tracks, the oncoming headlight
of a celestial train

God plays snare drums, horns
duel beneath sable clouds, cars
skid on steaming streets,
pedestrians scamper like
mice to dodge bullets of rain

Silver mists crown trees
almost black in the rainy
twilight, colors pure
as angels' eyes God moves in
the storm as well as sunlight

The twilight's from Poe:
gray scudding clouds, drizzling rain,
chill wind. He said you
liked me and I thought of your
smile and sunlight danced on Earth

I look at the cat
in late afternoon light. When
I die, will she find
a better human or fare
badly, alone on mean streets?

~Southern Indiana, USA

Andrew M Bowen lives in Indiana and has published about 87 poems. He is also an actor and an insurance agent.

Autumn Noelle Hall

shattered
in the first hailstorm
mom's victorian gazing ball
was never the way
to view the mountains

~Green Mountain Falls, Colorado, USA

casting a glance

Autumn Noelle Hall

   where white water boulder-slows into rock-bottom riffles cutthroat trout's blood-red blink caught in the aspen gold eye of an osprey as present in this moment as if he were present in this moment—

   reeling in
filaments of dawn
the stream exhales
a phantom fisherman
in the shape of my father

~Green Mountain Falls, Colorado, USA

For an indeterminate time—and much to her own surprise—Autumn Noelle Hall held the long distance record for watermelon seed spitting at Connor Prairie's Historical Village in Fishers, Indiana. She considers this irrefutable evidence that each of us has unnumbered hidden talents aching to be revealed. Her poetry is, among other things, an effort to encourage others to fearlessly (and despite juice dribbling down their chins) step up, because—ohhhh—discovery is sweet.

Bruce England

After his death,
there were days I thought
I should call him,
or he should call me, either
way, there were no calls

Alone in my home,
outside a great disturbance,
I went out to look,
stepping into the night,
leaving everything behind

I'm squatting
a croaking frog
fat-bellied
unwilling to jump
off my sofa-pad

Retired now,
I can't help but feel
like a beast
caught in the snare
of my condo

Above, transformed into tanka from "The Widow's Song," by Qernertoq in Eskimo Poems from Canada and Greenland, translated by Tom Lowenstein, 1973, pp 19-20.

The great sea stirs me,
sets me adrift, as a weed
in a great river,
the sky stirs me, the wind blows,
shakes my inward parts with joy

Above, a found and derived tanka from "The Great Sea," In the Trail of the Wind, by John Bierhorst (ed.); 1971, p. 124; translated from Inuit to Danish by Knud Rasmussen and from Danish to English by W. E. Calvert.

~Santa Clara, California, USA

Sedoka

Bruce England

In the future,
nature's hum will be
swarms of drones
pollinating
all the flowers
and fruit trees

I walk in beauty,
wandering in old age
on a trail of beauty,
lively may I walk,
long days may I walk, until
it is finished in beauty

Wounded soldier,
in a World War I film, shows
cigarette in hand nearly
covering his face,
lighting it, you can see him
inhale through a nostril

~Santa Clara, California, USA

Bruce England lives in Santa Clara, California, recently retired from library work. He's been writing Japanese-style poems for over thirty-five years. All that work is now a broad coalescence of poems into what is called The Great Complete.

Bryan Rickert

hotel lobby
an African woman's
work song
carrying me through
today's journey

hospital visit
in the bowels
of the research lab
a dying
office plant

saltwater tank
all the resources
and money
for one fish
that always hides

hospital garden
between tests
quiet
hosta leaves
cupping the dew

a foreman
barks orders
to immigrant men
in this patch of field
that once saw slaves

the hollow
bones of birds
since she's been gone
this feeling of never
being quite whole

twilight
answering the bullfrog's
call to prayer
the chorus rings out
through a cathedral of trees

sunset
snow shadows move
from black to blue
deepening in color
the last bruise you gave

done splashing
in puddles
a rook
carries fallen petals
back to the sky

funeral mass
the pew where she sat
for many years
showing the wear
of all those prayers

endless starlings
stretched
to the horizon
this funeral procession
on its way to the sea

a ball cap
absorbs the sweat
this June day
the crack of the bat
and the beer vender's cry

~Belleville, Illinois, USA

Bryan Rickert has been published in Frogpond, Modern Haiku, Acorn, Akitsu Quarterly, The Heron's Nest, Prune Juice, Failed Haiku, Contemporary Haibun Online, Atoms of Haiku III, Horizon: The Haiku Anthology, Taj Mahal Review, Atlas Poetica, Wales Haiku, Harvest of New Millennium and a number of other fine journals and anthologies. He is also the editor at The Living Senryu Anthology. His poetry collection "Fish Kite" is available through Cyberwit Publishing.

Toward Tomorrow

Carol Raisfeld

some days
the little girl in me
takes hold
nights with you
I am all woman

I know
your face by touch
in the dark
your breathing softer
when you are satisfied

only the clock
moving toward tomorrow
fills the silence
light from the street slips
through the shutters

times
when you smile
that way
I forget any sorrows
happy in your arms

the words
that worked wonders
don't anymore
but then sharing so much
we are a part of each other

at night
though miles away
I hear you sigh
seeing the moon is there
sad that you're all alone

and now
I try so hard to forget
you
yet hoping that you'll
come back to me

~*Atlantic Beach, New York, USA*

~*Century City, California, USA*

Change

Carol Raisfeld

happiness
meant I loved someone
knowing
they loved me back
when I was young

and now
as life moves on
happiness
is a slippery thing
peppered with love

it's not
wild colors or gifts
happiness
means my own personal
snow days with my lover

~*Atlantic Beach, New York, USA*

Transience

Carol Raisfeld

in loosening
the grip of grief
perhaps
love was on loan to me
from the universe

still
in dreams, my memory
replays
our intense sweetness
and the pain of parting

grateful
for having had love
in my life
I now know deep inside
the temporality of all things

~Greenwich Village, New York, USA

Sans Souci

Carol Raisfeld

at the boat shed
as we pull away the tarp
I remember
the flat water under a blue sky
wanting to sail 'round the world

early
each day getting to know
the boat again
and all the ways to ride
this freedom of the sea

years and miles
of sailing, it all comes
back to me
as things that are in
one's blood always do

~Santa Monica, California, USA

Passage

Carol Raisfeld

the meadows
rising and falling
wavelike
past my small room
the seasons float

bittersweet
memories of the past
rush in
I pack my belongings
for a last trip home

the candles
burned for just 24 hours
alone in my room
I cry when saying a prayer
for my parents

the moon
gives me childish comfort
tonight
the stars sweep down
to touch the horizon

~Santa Monica, California, USA

a red horizon
flanks the moon
I watch
the scattered stars
for a sign from you

icy cool
oysters on the half shell
slide down
shining your lips with
a silken saltiness

a full moon
across the pond
silence
but for the croaks
of mating frogs

in the hospice
she whispers "hold me"
and pressing
into the beat of my heart
she lets go

our last photo
I scissored him out
of my life . . .
at the funeral, locking eyes
with his young widow

light polishes
the surface of the sea
from a hidden beach
half in sun, half in shadow
you propose to me

make me a bird
and I shall sing for you
yet I yearn
to be a gentle river where
I float away your sorrows

meeting
in the cafe on a narrow street
at a table for two
with a slow grin he leans in
"I like to break rules"

my altered size
stiff limbs everywhere
his hunched gait
yet that smile and a wink
young lovers in disguise

opening
the window to spring
I cry. . .
birdsong fills the room
that held her life

our boat
rides rhythmic waves
into the night
across a path to the moon
. . . silver stars cluster

meeting
in the park that night
we shared secrets and promises
all forgotten
at dawn

sailing
no stars to guide me
at dawn
I look to the horizon
as wide as the sea

their spirits
brighten with the scent
of budding leaves . . .
this morning the dogs know
spring has begun

waiting
for my shadow
at moonrise . . .
these round river stones
older than our time together

winds of spring . . .
the nest spirals down
then a peep
followed by loud chirps
and a fluttering of wings

with a gentle sigh
the wind carries us
to a far cove
purple jellyfish umbrellas
float with the tide

the winds
sifting brittle leaves
to dust;
my last spring gone
with no one to care

~Playa Del Rey, California, USA

Kyoka

Carol Raisfeld

the train
speeds to the station
as crowds shift
eyes averted, swaying
breast to chest, he smiles

senior living
meeting new neighbors
with their son
THE DOCTOR
we couldn't be happier

stolen moments
holding each other close
again . . .
suddenly from downstairs
"Honey, I'm home!"

~Manhattan Beach, California

Carol Raisfeld lives in Atlantic Beach, a barrier island close to New York City. Her hobbies include sailing, chess, sculpting, painting and boxing. She holds US and foreign design patents in interactive soft toy design. Her poetry, art and photography appear worldwide in print, online journals and anthologies. Twitter: @carol_red.

Wind in Norwich — My Visit With Joy McCall

Carole Johnston

three witches
meander along ancient
Roman roads
one in wheelchair leads us
following wind blue stones

tower ruin
rooks gather here with wind
inside split rocks
jasper geode crowns
for the fairy queen

something
about to happen
with the wind
my indigo scarf dances
around my face

lunch
beneath the sacred
yew
we muse together
about death — how it hurts

we nibble
fairy food in the boneyard
drinking
potions from tiny magic
bottles feeling warm

she is
the Hawthorn Queen
wandering
along the hedgerows
my heart follows

where she goes
grasses part in wonder
paths open
wind and sky sing
her name

a fairy ring
appears for us
she says
"witches dance" so we dance
blessed be the wind

even
as we leave
this place
her song in my mind
"It is well with my soul"

~Hawes Green, Norwich, England

Carole Johnston

day I left
crow called from a
hidden branch
where no crow has been before
call to adventure

~Lexington, Kentucky

pilgrimage
riding trains in Scotland
searching
for ancient magic here
among standing stones

~outside Edinburgh, Scotland

ancient
cairns sleeping
stones
moss covered
sun glittered

~Clava Cairns, Inverness, Scotland

window watching
trains roll over green
hills
mesmerized
I become magic

~Yorkshire Downs, England

hopping off
the train at Penrith
first moment
there's a castle
crows in the ruins

~Penrith, England

Stonehenge
I stand alone among
crowds
nothing matters but
eons of stars

~Stonehenge, England

Carole Johnston lives and writes in Lexington, Kentucky where she is a free lance teacher. She has published two books of tanka and haiku, "Journeys:Getting Lost," and "Manic Dawn."

Chen-ou Liu

the flight path
of a monarch butterfly . . .
to stay or to go
stretching the silence
among migrants

~*Burlington, Ontario, Canada*

crammed
shoulder to shoulder
factory girls
pump their tired hands, shouting
Bread and Roses!

tires screech
when making a sharp turn
a young man
yells *Go to hell!*
at the hearse driver

she bites
her bottom lip —
I leave
my broken promise
inside her

~*Toronto, Ontario, Canada*

sleepless
on this summer solstice
tomorrow
the night will lengthen
my loneliness, too

this attic
I've lived in for ten years
silent now
the night and I
grow older and darker

such humid heat
and not a word penned . . .
my dog and I
stare at the emptiness
of this dull afternoon

I try to call her
but hang up the phone
before it rings . . .
the silence between us
becomes thicker and darker

~*Ajax, Ontario, Canada*

lying on top
my crush looks at me
and blushes . . .
summer grass holds the shape
of our first night together

~*Taipei, Taiwan*

a Pacific breeze
brushing across my face
I breathe in
the scent of my mother,
an ocean away

~*Vancouver, British Columbia, Canada*

Chen-ou Liu lives in Ajax, Ontario, Canada. He is the author of five books, including Following the Moon to the Maple Land (First Prize, 2011 Haiku Pix Chapbook Contest) and A Life in Transition and Translation (Honorable Mention, 2014 Turtle Light Press Biennial Haiku Chapbook Competition), His tanka and haiku have been honored with many awards.

Chris Bullard lives in Philadelphia, PA. He received his B.A. in English from the University of Pennsylvania and his M.F.A. from Wilkes University. Finishing Line Press published his poetry chapbook, Leviathan, in 2016 and Kattywompus Press published High Pulp, a collection of his flash fiction, in 2017. His work has appeared in recent issues of Nimrod, Muse/A Journal, The Woven Tale, Red Coyote, Cutthroat and The Offbeat.

Cullen Whisenhunt is a recent graduate of Oklahoma City University's Red Earth Creative Writing MFA program, and he lives and writes in Durant, Oklahoma (US). His poetry has been published in Frogpond, Ninth Letter, The Ekphrastic Review, Red River Review, and Dragon Poet Review, among others.

Waiting for the Eulogy

Chris Bullard

My friends have acted
with amazing discretion
by their absolute
refusal to flatter me
in the least until I'm dead.

~United States

Statuary Sequence

Cullen Whisenhunt

for Keely Record

four-foot flamingo
rusting at the seams
dances with nature
beside butterflies
big as barn owls

two concrete children,
arms crossed, tilted
into the same tree, counting
an eternal game
of hide-and-seek

stone squirrel
with prayer-clasped paws—
above, acorns ripen

angels, saints, the virgin
Mary, and Jesus himself
with backs turned, casting
the first shadows—
long, deep, dark

~Durant, Oklahoma, USA

Dave Read

she says
that I don't clean
enough:
another
polished poem

typing
another poem
online
my day slips
into my phone

teased and gelled
like it's 1984
her hair
holds firm
to the past

crushing
an empty can
of Coke . . .
the night folds in
on autumn

stuffing
the suitcase with
dirty clothes
I shut the lid
on summer

light
refracting in
the mist
a bag of rainbow
Skittles

~Calgary, Alberta, Canada

Flight

Dave Read

trying
to book my flight
online
my passport
has expired

nearly midnight
and everything's
closed—
shadows split
the open blinds

hoping
to visit the land
of the free
I find myself
tied up

unable to sleep
I'm the first
to arrive
at the government
services office

three hundred dollars
for a rush order—
I adjust
my travel
budget

my cabbie
speeds through
downtown traffic
his words rush
past my ears

arriving
for my flight
on time
I settle in
for a selfie

~*Calgary, Alberta, Canada*

Lopsided

Dave Read

keeping me
up to speed
on the game
my wife's high-five
emoji

late afternoon,
the game winds down . . .
a shadow
the length of
the pitch

after she tells him
not to give up
a crack
in the tone
of her voice

on the wrong side
of a lopsided game
the boys
shove the loss
in their backpacks

stuck in
the consolation
round
the team plays out
its weekend

~*Calgary, Alberta, Canada*

Dave Read is a Canadian poet living in Calgary. He primarily writes short poems with an emphasis on the Japanese forms of tanka, haiku, and haibun.

pistil and stamen

Debbie Strange

evening wind
heavy with the perfume
of sweet peas
we are tendrils clinging
to each other's heart

sunflowers
from a market stall
we warm
ourselves with memories
of happier times

I shower
you with petals
this ceremony
the simple hallmark
of mourning

my garden
is wizened now
but soon
it will be plump
and ripe with snow

~*Winnipeg, Manitoba, Canada*

Debbie Strange (Winnipeg, Manitoba, Canada) is a short form poet, photographer, and haiga artist. She is a member of the Manitoba Writers' Guild and is also affiliated with several haiku and tanka organizations. Her first collection, Warp and Weft: Tanka Threads was published by Keibooks in 2015, and the sequel, Three-Part Harmony: Tanka Verses was released by Keibooks in 2018. Debbie maintains a publication archive at https://debbiemstrange.blogspot.com/ and tweets @Debbie_Strange.

Elisa Theriana

Elisa Theriana, Indonesian-English Translator

Terjemahan Inggris-Indonesia oleh Elisa Theriana

fresh flowers
on the old scars
every Christmas
we recite
memories of dad

bunga segar
di atas luka lama
setiap Natal
mengulang cerita
tentang ayah

end of summer
the mosquitoes
with a new song
her smile
still eludes me

musim panas berlalu
nyamuk nyamuk
mendengungkan lagu baru
senyum gadis itu
masih tak tergapai

spring star
as if we were one
his first hiccup
pulls
my heartbeat

bintang musim semi
seakan kita satu
buah hati tersedu
menyentak
degup jantungku

nine
little black birds
perch on the power line
how can I tell
one from the others

sembilan
burung hitam kecil
bertengger di kabel listrik
dapatkah kubedakan
satu dengan lainnya

dissecting
a rose
petal by petal
the scarlet letter
of her old tattoo

merepih
sekuntum mawar
kelopak berguguran
rajah si gadis
merah membara

hey, stars . . .
stop trying
as if loneliness
needs
a reason

oh, bintang. . .
berhenti berharap
seakan sepi ini
perlu
alasan

~Bandung, Indonesia

Elisa Theriana from Bandung, Indonesia, works as a computer programmer. a haiku and tanka lover, also a photography enthusiast.

Elisa Theriana berasal dari Bandung, Indonesia. Sehari hari bekerja sebagai programer komputer. Pecinta haiku, tanka dan penggiat fotografi.

Elizabeth Howard

in winter's freezes
the old snapping turtle sleeps
in creek mud . . .
when a gentle zephyr whispers
he begins to rise

smoldering brush
    erupts
engulfs the school . . .
all of our knowledge
ashes blowing in the wind

the stately buck
with a castle on his head
strides down the sward . . .
all other bucks
give way

uncle a scholar born
sentenced to a lifetime
plowing corn, slopping hogs,
lifting bales of hay
he wears a scowl

the old bucks
skirmish
for fallen peaches
antlers clashing
in the swirling fog

like a goose lost in the flyway
I cry out in the dark night
and then comes the light . . .
I settle on the river of peace
where he waits for me

friend's cell phone
her new cancer number
as she crumples
I see my daughter's
distraught face

Hate spreads
like bindweed
insidious
delusive
bent on annihilation

in her attic
a worn carpetbag
bulging with sepia photographs
everyone
anonymous

a pregnant doe
at the window . . .
after all these years
I recall a butterfly
in my rib cage

breast center
she doodles
on a scrap of paper
tangled vines
run amok

he flees through the swamp
a quagmire of cypress knees
muck sucks his shoes
mosquitos eat his ears
he bursts into tears

~Tennessee, USA

Back against the Wall

Elizabeth Howard

Hands frozen,
back against the wall,
I watch a covey of cops
convey a young man
to the psych ward.

They tote him
in a straitjacket, a deer,
no, a rabid wolf,
spitting, foaming,
howling.

Hot, cold, dizzy,
I cannot move
when a red-faced cop
points a cudgel at me
yelling, *Back!*

Had I words
And breath enough
I would tell him
my back's
against the wall.

How can I go back?
unsee what I've seen,
the face of this boy,
helpless but for his mouth,
the voices spilling out.

As they rush away
the boy lashes his head,
his face twists,
and for a suffocating moment
becomes my son's.

~Tennessee, USA

Elizabeth Howard lives in Arlington, Tennessee. Her tanka have been published in Eucalypt, red lights, Mariposa, Ribbons, Gusts, Atlas Poetica, Skylark, Moonbathing, and other journals.

tankaku

Fractled

out of reach
awash in sin
a prayer
for the lost souls
connected to mine

guiding light
the body of moths
by daybreak

if anything
you can call
me that nobody
who is made
of stardust

the Milky Way
a telescope finds
more pixels

not hungry
to my disgust
a full bowl
looks the same
with each bite

housecleaning
a hurricane sweeps
into the dust pan

thunder rattles
my window
the silence
I now appreciate
with ringing ears

lightning show
the scrambled wordplay
of an argument

a sliver
of twilight left
on wounds
left wide open
the night gapes

fresh snow—
flashes of gunfire
on a blood trail

half full
that's beyond distance
while longing
to touch her again
only a dream will allow

half empty
the bright side
of the moon

falling in love
the sudden youth
to feel again
a butterfly swarm
while over the hill

new relationship
the long distance
via age gap

another dream
about flight
recurring
to greet everyone
as a crow

an omen
this harvest moon
more death

falling leaves
on this autumn day
another sign
as each day passes
where we part as well

first snowfall
nothing but bare trees
and cold words to bare

afternoon fog
the beauty of it all
while eyes dilate
to see light glimmer
brighter in darkness

autumn sky
a veil lifts away
with the wind

~New York, USA

Fractled, under the great mentorship and friend, Brendon Kent and a member of "The Haiku Nook" still dabbling with haiku and its related forms while encountering entities with extreme knowledge of such poetic forms. Published in numerous journals. Fractled is also experimental with his work who created the first published sequence/parallel haiku while hoping to find a home for other experiments such as "tankaku" "kyokaku" and "hashtagku". Fractled currently resides in the USA, NY.

Gabriel Martins

blue skies and grey clouds
  one drifting on the other
    the wind comes in time
      I firmly hold your cold hand
        wondering if fate likes us

Waves crash at the beach
  bringing and taking new things
    as I watch calmly
      our lives heading to new paths
        are they going to seek the same

Lost
  The morning sun shines
    the air is getting hotter
      my breath goes slower
        as the sight of you warms me
          my heart pounds fast in my chest

Small thunders inside
  as the sun is bright outside
    the blue fills me up
      of my routine and PC
        my boredom fills the morning

cold winds in early mornings
  missing summer dearly
    it keeps moving forward
      i feel lost at my table
        wondering if summer is going to arrive

~Brazil

Gabriel Martins is a linguistics graduate, working as a translator at an office job, he lives in Campinas, Brazil, he loves dogs, jazz and his girlfriend.

Gail Brooks

it rains
every afternoon
a canoe
could navigate the waters
rushing down the cobblestone streets

~A summer storm in San Miguel de Allende, Mexico

someone
has to buy the art
try on clothes
eat at new restaurants
else we'd all be poor

~An afternoon in the village of Laguna Beach, California, USA

everything was grey
on the street where I lived
in 1945
the houses, the lawns, the streets
but not the pink hollyhocks on the fence

~Vermont Street in Detroit, Michigan, USA. The street no longer exists.

they took pieces
of my breast and my stomach
finding my mortality
what they couldn't take
was my hopefulness

~Recent stomach biopsy, Hoag Hospital, Newport Beach, California, USA

Gail Brooks is a retired university executive with degrees in labor relations and law and inching slowly to older age. My inspiration comes first from my family and friends and then from the wonders of travel.

Okane

Genie Nakano

Money money money
How much do you make
How much can you take
beads, sugar and spices
let's trade with good will

Ask a person
how much money do you make
it's unpresidential
or "How old are you"
impolite—crude and crass

My income—
Retirement—450 dollars a month
Social Security
It's all so boring and petty
I'm 71 and moving up

A billionaire friend of mine
asked what's this issue about money
can we travel
on higher ground
don't let your dog poop on my lawn

It's only money
lying, dying, crying
craving
a paper moon
let's stir a melting pot

A stranger came to town
claiming he could make soup
from a rusty nail
(a childhood story I recall)
then everyone pitched in . . .

Onions from one
potatoes from another
one small carrot
wild herbs growing on the grounds
on and on . . . in the end a feast . . .

~California, USA

Genie Nakano lives in Gardena, CA, where she teaches yoga and dance at the Japanese Cultural Center of Gardena. She has a regular column for the Rafu Shimpo where she shares her tanka and short stories. She has written three books of tanka available on Amazon.Com and can be reached at enieYogini@Yahoo.Com.

Pre-Raphaelite Girls

Gerry Jacobson

Janey stares
out of her gilt frame
modelling
the goddess of love . . .
would she look after *me*?

D. G. Rossetti, Astarte Syriaca, 1877. Oil on canvas, Manchester Art Gallery.

a young woman drifts
in an ornate canoe
I notice
the intricate brushwork
of his candles and bullrushes

J.W. Waterhouse, The Lady of Shalott, 1888. Oil on canvas, Tate Britain.

I'll be there
in apple blossom time . . .
pre-Raphaelite girls
with long red hair
are sipping cream

J. E. Millais, Apple Blossoms, 1858–9. Oil on canvas, Lady Lever Art Gallery, Port Sunlight, UK.

Dante Gabriel
draws his sister
downcast
trying to rhyme
her next sonnet sequence

D. G. Rossetti, Christina Rossetti, 1877. Pastel on paper, private collection, Melbourne.

the knight
with clanging metal thighs
looks up . . .
La belle Dame sans Merci
has stolen his sword

Arthur Hughes, La Belle Dame sans Merci, 1863. Oil on canvas, National Gallery of Victoria.

pretty lady
in a pale blue dress
selling
her empty purse
with its double meaning

James Colinson, The Empty Purse, 1857. Oil on canvas, Tate Britain.

'fallen woman'
brushes her long red hair
in poverty
outside her window
the city stinks

John R. S. Stanhope, Thoughts of the Past, 1858–9. Oil on canvas, Tate Britain.

the strain
shows on Effie's face
as she
obtains her divorce
and marries the artist

J. E. Millais, The Order of Release, 1746. 1852–9. Oil on canvas, Tate Britain.

Miss Siddel
models for Millais
in the bath
as mad Ophelia
she catches a cold

J. E. Millais, Ophelia, 1851-2. Oil on canvas, Tate Britain.

the crucifix
is a rack of chisels
but Hunt's Christ
with long red hair and beard
is a stunning beauty

William Holman Hunt, The Shadow of Death, 1870. Oil on canvas, Manchester Art Gallery.

~Paintings and drawings in the exhibition 'Love and Desire'. National Gallery of Australia, Canberra, 2019.

The Year I Was Born

Gerry Jacobson

    grey dawn
    stretching, bending
    today
    shall be my dancing day
    tears in my eyes

I was born in 1939, that fateful year. Along with 1914, the most fateful year of that lost and bloody century. The outbreak of the Second World War. Which now seems to have followed on from the First World War; with just a twenty-year gap of "peace".

    embraced
    by the soundscape
    going deep within
    moving in space
    dancing through time

My birthday was 13th July, just seven weeks before war broke out. So I was conceived in October 1938, the time of the Munich crisis, when Czechoslovakia was fed to a pack of wolves. And November 1938 was the month of *Kristallnacht* when 30 000 Jews were imprisoned in Germany, and most of the synagogues and Jewish-owned businesses were trashed.

    what is that large bird
    perched on my shoulder
    in a dream
    trying desperately
    to shake it off

I've always known a deep-seated fear. It manifests as shyness, a reluctance to speak out or confront people, and an avoidance of authority figures. It's nothing to do with my everyday life. Inherited perhaps, like in ancestral genes? Or passed on by my mother, *in utero* or in my early childhood? She would have been anxious during her pregnancy.

    what colour
    is my fear today . . .
    black like the space
    behind closed eyes
    or red like morning traffic lights?

She had been in England for five years as a refugee from Nazi Germany. Her parents and other relatives and friends were still over there, trapped by the Nazi clampdown on Jewish life and emigration, and the confiscation of assets. I remember how she cursed the Nazis. Hitler was *"Der Mamzer!"* But that was later when she knew her parents had been murdered.

    please come to me
    dear sensations
    and emotions
    let me hold you
    then let you go

The war started on 3rd September 1939 though nothing much happened for a while in England. I believe that I was evacuated with my mother to Leicestershire. I don't know if it was at the outbreak of war, or the following year when London was bombed. A village name is half-buried in my memory — Fleckley, Flenley — something like that. I wonder how it was for that young German-Jewish refugee with her baby, billeted in country England of 1939–40. And how was it for Baby?

    with hooded eyes
    we mingle and walk
    occasionally
    touching, then diverting
    how brief our stay

    ~England

Gerry Jacobson lives in Yarralumla, a Canberra suburb, and may often be found in its cafes. He journals in tanka and blogs (on facebook) in tanka prose. He once was a geologist. Gerry dotes on four young grandchildren and visits them in Sydney and in Stockholm.

Grunge, M. Kei, and the Random Poetry Generator

Grunge and M. Kei discovered a tanka poetry generator online and decided to see what it would produce. These are some of the tanka it created. The results are presented without comment.

the clotting of her
a nightjar in a tree screams
a tissues of lies
the ghastly centre of her
trapped in the constellations

engines left to rot
his false shadow, painted skin
ocean above sky
grey hide in the undergrowth
gold ice reindeer on the porch

trucks carve the valley
flame smears of shrunken pumpkins
wide flat dusty road
empty crossings on corners
forest deer culled by the road

trucks carve the valley
hyena cry in the trees
tar black feather ball
forest deer culled by the road
she is stardust she is earth

~Internet

M. Kei is a tall ship sailor and award-winning poet who lives on Maryland's Eastern Shore. He is the editor of Atlas Poetica : A Journal of World Tanka, and Stacking Stones, An Anthology of Short Tanka Sequences. His most recent collection of poetry is January, A Tanka Diary. He is also the author of the award-winning gay Age of Sail adventure novels, Pirates of the Narrow Seas (http://www.atlaspoetica.org/buy-novels/). He can be followed on Twitter @kujakupoet, or visit AtlasPoetica.org.

Grunge lives in South Florida with too many cats. Send help.

The Random Poetry Generator automatically creates randomly generated computer poetry. The poem generator works by randomly selecting from hundreds of lines of poetry of different syllable lengths to generate a short structured poem. It currently generates haikus, tankas, lanternes, nonets, quinzaines, katautas, sedokas, and clarity pyramids. The generator is founded on the principle of "1000 monkeys for 1000 years eventually producing the works of Shakespeare." https://www.namegeneratorfun.com/poetry.

Geoffrey Winch is a retired engineer residing on the English south coast. He is associated with several local creative writing groups for who he devises and leads occasional workshops. He writes free form poetry in addition to tanka, tanka prose, haiku, haibun and cherita; and reads regularly at Chichester Open Mic. Author of five collections, his most recent being a pamphlet, West Abutment Mirror Images, published by Original Plus in 2017.

Geoffrey Winch

that day
our lips met briefly
then the question was
would they ever
meet again

~Reading, UK

holding her hand again
after it's been held by
so many others
getting a grip on
our pasts and future

~Chawton, UK

Armchair Travel

Hema Ravi

For the inmates of the seniors home, there are entertainment programmes, discussions, friendly chats, yoga and more. Most individuals indulge in chats with virtual people. A few go for a stroll in the green environs around, that is home to the peacocks and several other species.

The gentle drone of the fan is the discordant sound in the quiet room where the aged man sits with a religious book.

> butterfly at window
> flies off
> is that
> a sign
> of someone coming

Five years have passed since he came here. Not wanting to be a burden on his son, he had moved over to this place after the demise of his beloved life partner.

> blissful solitude
> watching
> bees collecting nectar
> as autumn clouds
> gather

~India

Hema Ravi is a freelance trainer for IELTS and Communicative English. Her poetic publications include haiku, tanka, free verse and metrical verses. Her write ups have been published in the Hindu, New Indian Express, Femina, Woman's Era and several online and print journals; a few haiku and form poems have been prize winners. She is a permanent contributor to the 'Destine Literare' (Canada). She is the author of 'Everyday English,' 'Write Right Handwriting Series 1, 2, 3,' co-author of Sing Along Indian Rhymes' and 'Everyday Hindi.'

Hemapriya Chellappan

the scent
of your shampoo
lingers on my fingers
sometimes, travelling light
can be heavy

midday heat
a snake slithers out
of earth's fissure
sometimes when no one's
watching, I pick my nose

far away from home
my hopes and dreams
shattered on the floor
empty pizza boxes
in a dimly lit room

an ancient fort
on a mountaintop
I take refuge
in my shadow
gathering dust

the electric hum
of the refrigerator
a mouse
I can't find hides
under my bed

~Chennai, India

Hemapriya Chellappan is a haikai poet, illustrator and haiga artist who resides in Pune, India. She took to Japanese literary short forms in the summer of 2019. Ever since her works have been published in various international print journals and e-magazines including The Heron's Nest, Hedgerow, Acorn, Prune Juice and other notable publications. Her work has also appeared in Living Senryu Anthology and podcasts. When she isn't daydreaming she writes jokes, sketches landscapes, hums old songs and makes excellent tea.

Crayfish

Ignatius Fay

forbidden
to go near the river
we strip
sure of dry clothes
to wear home

we wade
into the frigid water
stripped to underwear
steps tentative
on slimy boulders

how long
we can bear the cold
the challenge
to stay upright
against the numbing current

a slip
almost swept away
close call
laughed about
as we dry in the sun

Monday morning
absent from school
a friend
drowned Saturday
catching crayfish

~Levack, Ontario, Canada

Open Road

Ignatius Fay

I have been on 24-hour oxygen therapy for more than a year. A portable oxygen tank allows me to go out, if for no other reason than to drive my classic '65 Mustang. When I am up to it, of course.

disorientation
loss of concentration
first signs
of falling oxygen levels
hypoxia

Saturday afternoon, driving my teenaged daughters to the beach. The older exclaims, 'Dad! You just ran that red light!'

Confused and shaken, I pull over. Not only did I not see the light, I wasn't even aware of the intersection. An intersection I've used much of my driving life. The rest of the drive is slow and long.

Tuesday, the next week. I pick the girls up at school. Different intersection; same scenario.

facing
the decision
give up my license
before I hurt someone
or that car

~Sudbury, Ontario, Canada

Fire In The Hole

Ignatius Fay

My father-in-law is uneducated. He also lacks judgment and common sense and has a tendency to act without thinking. To make matters worse, he drinks too much.

We're at his cottage for the weekend. An old logging camp, it has a main building for his immediate family and several smaller buildings for his daughters and their husbands, or other relatives and friends who stop by.

Sunday afternoon. He is quite inebriated. His wife has been nagging him all weekend.

    over-full
    offensive to eyes and nose
    outhouse
    his months-old promise
    to dig a new one

He flees the kitchen and her relentless tirade. Beer and cigar in hand, and without a word to anyone, he crosses the courtyard to a small shed where he stores materials used in his stone quarry. From there, stopping first to take a slug of beer, he enters the old outhouse. Moments later, he is again crossing the courtyard, in no apparent hurry, when the dynamite goes off and the outhouse erupts.

    ground rumbles
    windows rattle
    everywhere
    a turmoil of poop, wood splinters
    and wadded toilet paper

While debris is still hitting the ground, he shouts for his son, Jr, until the teenager steps out of the main building.

'Tell your mom I dealt with the outhouse, then get out here and start digging the new hole.'

    labor day
    outhouse not yet built
    family reunion
    empty the chamber pot
    into the hole

~Lake Nipissing, Ontario, Canada

First Date

Ignatius Fay

Trying to impress her on our first date, I take her to the most expensive restaurant I can afford. She is so pretty in her delicate yellow summer dress. I don't know if she is nervous, but I certainly am. We have a number of similar interests, though, so the conversation is going well.

We pause a moment to order, then back to our discussion of Disney cartoons. As is my habit, I am gesticulating to emphasize what I am saying. While making a particularly important point, my hand knocks her large, untouched glass of water into her lap. The entire front of her dress is soaked and the pale yellow has become transparent. Stupidly, I grab a napkin and dab at the sopping cloth most inappropriately. Things go downhill from there.

    still, surprise!
    she marries me
    another sunny day
    that goes well
    until it doesn't

~Sudbury, Ontario, Canada

Ignatius Fay

at the bus stop
the girl I'm sweet on
chance meeting
after having been
to the same Disney movie

under the raincoat
down my neck
cold rain
all the dandelions
closed for the day

in the closet
dad's old geological
hammer
next to his spare
oxygen tank

honestly
despite what I told her
when I left
it was her
not me

the meal
we always ate together
breakfast
now a coffee
in the car

self-checkout
when did I become
an employee?
now — if the store
offered a discount . . .

in the terrarium
next to my wife
a large stuffed iguana
until it moves
and she freaks

night nurse
on the cardiac ward
twelve-hour shift
talking much too quickly
after the energy drink

~Sudbury, Ontario, Canada

Ignatius a retired invertebrate paleontologist, writes haiku, tanka, haibun, tanka prose and rengay. His poems have appeared in many of the most respected online and print journals. In 2012, he co-authored a collection of poems, entitled Breccia, with Irene Golas. He is the current editor of the Haiku Society of America Bulletin and does the layout for the HSA's journal frogpond. Ignatius resides in Sudbury, Ontario, Canada.

Jackie Chou

cooling air
in mid-October
warm breezes
whispering
their last secrets

reaching
out the window
to feel the rain
a poem grows
from my palms

my childhood
staring at the ceiling
water stains
became a menagerie
of animal shapes

morning patio
benches once peopled
now empty
where yesterday's words
and cigarettes linger

fighting the voices
of a mental disorder
a young me
slips further away
every passing day

fallen feathers
was it a mystery bird
or an angel
trespassing in the night
when we all slumbered

~*Southern California, USA*

Jason Morgan

Breath from the cold north
among clouds your wings descend
horse hooves pound the air
from the mount you seized your bride
and begat a girl of snow.

The candle freezes
and teacups lay in pieces
the skylark sings on
eternity stretches more
leaving room for graveyard ice.

Storm, where is your home?
among the clouds where rain weeps
mourning the dead sun
as lightning leaps and cuts air
while the world awaits your exit?

~*Sydney, Australia*

My name Jason Morgan and I live in Sydney, New South Wales, Australia. Writing poetry helps me to see the world through fresh eyes. Poetry allows us to tell a story in a personal, philosophical way which captures the cadence of language. Writing verse allows me time to synthesize experience. I hope you enjoy my works.

Jackie Chou is a poet residing in sunny Southern California. She sometimes gets her inspirations from common city birds and flowers. Her works have been published in Atlas Poetica, Skylark, Ribbons, the cherita journal, moonbathing, ephemerae, and others.

Cherita

Joanna Ashwell

winding down

to the evenings
long shadows

where a doorway
finds new ways
to entice you

it's sad but true

while you're
still out there

I don't
feel safe
anywhere

one last flight

between us
where we meet

in the crest
of dawn and dew
winnowing our limbs

the dandelion

full of sunlight
and hope

where our wishes
land softly
upon the wind

I grow alarmed

as your words
take shape between us

you're all charms
rattling a stick
at emptiness

somewhere
between
the next axe

I slip away
untethered

tiptoeing upon the stars

starlings

I release you
at twilight

the murmuration
the many shapes
of our love

untouchable

as a rainbow
beyond us

always drifting
over and away
the unreachable arc

~United Kingdom

Joanna Ashwell, a writer from the North East of England. Published in various journals for haiku, tanka, haibun and cherita. Enjoys observing all the seasons and fortunately prefers autumn and winter to the summer - summer doesn't always happen in the UK

John Zheng

moon through clouds
a dreamboat
sailing home
    always there
    always not there

waiting for mail
on the porch
the woman cuddles her cat
love in her arms
in her memory

spring wind
her nostrils quiver
before a sneeze
the whole class responds:
god bless you

winter dawn
the blinds admit
a dim light
a faint chirp
of a baby bird

pair calling—
a cardinal's eager sound
from a sweet maple
half over the roof
a blinking sunrise

~Mississippi, USA

John Zheng (Itta Bena, Mississippi) has published haiku, haibun, and tanka in Haibun Today, Contemporary Haibun, Frogpond, Ribbons, Asahi Haiku, Mainichi Haiku, Chrysanthemum among other publications. He teaches at Mississippi Valley State University.

Choka

Joshua Michael Stewart

The cat's been out all night
and just as I start to think
that this may be it, that this
may be the beginning
of never again, she comes
scratching at the window.

November's damp gray
weighs heavy on pine branches
and on mind and heart.
But also cold and fragile,
the oak's red leaves still cling.

~Ware, Massachusetts, USA

Po Chu-i Golden Shovel Tanka

Joshua Michael Stewart

yellow leaves
drop into the river
flow over the falls
you've been gone ten years
our love gone longer

~Mill River, Florence, Massachusetts, USA

burning brush pile
flame-paints our shadows
against the house
smoke reaches
for night's first star

~Spencer, Massachusetts, USA

Cherita

Joshua Michael Stewart

summers on grandma's farm
a rusted-out pickup
at the cornfield's edge
we'd throw rocks
at boredom

~Manchester, Ohio, USA

---

winter evening
full moon in the sky
you've been gone since may
what is it that you bring
across fields of snow

three days
I've shaken my keys
called the cat's name
heavy clouds refuse
to release the rain

inside a tulip bulb
a bumblebee
my love sticks
their tongue
in my ear

after spring rain
the crow's caw
sleek and clean
near a rotting stump
a white flower

~Ware, Massachusetts, USA

---

confession

she tucks
the revolver
into her purse

as she climbs
the church steps

---

the moon stares

at me like a child
holding a cereal box

when I look up
I'm diving
into a bowl of milk

---

lawnmower
in the distance

I yearn for what I can't name

but I know
it's name
is not yard work

~Ware, Massachusetts, USA

Double Cherita

Joshua Michael Stewart

mother's day

the disease
has taken her voice

through the phone
her quick breath
nursing home clatter

morning
rain

deleting
my mother's
number

out of my phone

~Ware, Massachusetts, USA

Joshua Michael Stewart grew up in Sandusky, Ohio, but now lives in Ware, Massachusetts. He has had poems published in the Massachusetts Review, Salamander, Modern Haiku, Frogpond, Brilliant Corners, and many others. His first full-length collection of poems, Break Every String, was published by Hedgerow Books in 2016.

Jakob

Joy McCall

 A man was at my door when I got home from the clinic and I didn't know at first who he was — Norwich is a place with a fair mix of good and evil.
 It pays to be a little wary; especially for a crippled woman like me.

he was huge
shaven head
piercings
wild black tattoos
on his body

 Scary. But when he saw me coming along the path, he said — 'lady, I help you?' and held out a parcel.
 I have learned not to judge a book by its cover. Covers can deceive.
 He didn't speak much English but we talked a bit.
 He showed me his tattoos — ancient Maori symbols he had done in Australia. Full arm sleeves, full legs and neck. Strangely beautiful.
 I asked why he was in Norwich doing what is hard work delivery driving — minimum wage and they have to use their own cars.
 He said he is working all over the world to try and find the real meaning of life before he settles down somewhere.
 He came to Norwich from Slovakia because he read that there are more good tattoo parlours in this city than anywhere in Europe.

he stays awhile
in one place
musing on life
but doesn't find an answer
and moves on

 He has left a tattoo space over his heart for when he does find the answer.

I said—
maybe
the meaning
is not outside
but within

 He asked if he could sit on my doorstep and think.
 So I left him there and he was there a long time and then gone—but he left the parcel he was to deliver on the step,
 and he had written on the top in scrawled black ink capitals 'THANK YOU LADY'.

 It made me cry. Somehow those encounters make up for a lot of my day-to-day suffering.

I wonder
where he will go to now?
maybe
the place doesn't matter
so much any more

~*Norwich, England*

The book launch

Joy McCall

for Saul and Bill Albert

 The old vaulted room was filled with chattering people.

 A string quartet was playing popular songs in the open courtyard where they served wine and coffee and cake.

 The dying poet sat old and still in his wheelchair, his constant carer at his side.

 The young man with long hair and dragon tattoos was reading some of the poems aloud.

 The crowd clapped. The old poet smiled.

 Another young man stood behind the old man, his hand on his shoulder, tears in his dark eyes.

in the midst
of noise and chatter
a quiet song—
the love of a man
for his father

~*Norwich, England*

Joy McCall has only ever been to one poetry reading in her life— the new one for the book the Beauty of Rust, tanka written with Bill Albert, Illustrated by Paul Levy. It was held in an ancient old building in the city centre. These things are hard work for her, but it was made wonderful by seeing the son and the father and the love between them. Nothing else mattered.

far, far away

Joy McCall

While strange heatwaves and summer storms break over Norwich, on the remote border of Finland and Russia, it is bitterly cold.

My nomad friend is tired and hungry.

Even in summer, icy winds are blowing.

It's many miles to any food store, much too far to walk and there are no passable roads through the vast forest.

he wanders out
on the frozen White Sea
dragging a branch
and makes a fire to cook
a small rabbit and a fish

He eats whatever he happens to find in the forest or on the shore.

He makes his cook-fires on the sea so as not to set the forest alight.

The ice is so thick it doesn't melt.

~Norwich, England

five years on

Joy McCall & Margaret Knapke

for Brian Zimmer, d. November 5, 2014

*five years on
and still I miss him
and the madness
that was closer to beauty
than sanity could ever be*

brother beyond blood,
beyond breath but never love,
I look to the moon
and feel *mi hermano*
contemplating starry paths

*it is enough
to have found the words
and set them alight
in the middle of a wood
where the stars hear them crackle*
— Brian Zimmer

even when the sky
is lit with myriad stars
there's a black hole
where his smile, his words
used to shine

darkness holds stars and roots,
silence releases thunder,
holds birdsong aloft.
his old typewriter for haiku—
nothing can redeem its stillness

~England / Dayton, Ohio, USA

Margaret Knapke is an infrequent poet who had the great pleasure of writing rengay with her dear, longtime friend Brian Zimmer. They shared passions for El Día de Muertos / Day of the Dead, human-rights activism, animals, and mystical inquiry. And they frequently laughed themselves to tears.

Joy McCall and Margaret Knapke still feel sadness at the loss of such a good friend and fine poet. Rest in Peace, dear Brian.

Tan-Renga

Karen O'Leary & Paul Callus

Paul Callus, English — Maltese-English Translator

Paul Callus, Traduttur Ingliż — Malti

s h a t t e r e d pot
the dust and water used
to make clay

forgiveness and dialogue
heal moments of weakness

bieqja m f a r r k a
it-trab u l-ilma
li jsawru t-tafal

maħfra u djalogu
ifejqu waqtiet ta' dgħufija

~*West Fargo, North Dakota, USA / Ħal Safi, Malta*

moist clay takes shape
under a potter's
skillful hands . . .

*my homemade cards
extend the experience*

tafal niedi jieħu l-għamla
fl-idejn imħarrġa
ta' fuħħari . . .

*il-kartolini li naghmel
ikabbru l-esperjenza*

~*Ħal Safi, Malta / West Fargo, North Dakota, USA*

Karen O'Leary is a writer and editor from West Fargo, North Dakota in The United States of America. She has published poetry, short stories, and articles in a variety of venues including, Frogpond, A Hundred Gourds, bear creek haiku, Shemom, Creative Inspirations, Bamboo Hut, and NeverEnding Story. She edited an international online journal called 'Whispers' <http://whispersinthewind333.blogspot.com> for 5½ years. She enjoys sharing the gift of words.

Karen O'Leary hija awtriċi u editriċi minn West Fargo, North Dakota fl-Istati Uniti tal-Amerika. Hija ppubblikat poeżiji, stejjer qosra, u artikli f'diversi siti, fosthom Frogpond, A Hundred Gourds, bear creek haiku, Shemom, Creative Inspirations, Bamboo Hut, u NeverEnding Story. Għal 5½ snin kienet l-editriċi tal-ġurnal internazzjonali online 'Whispers' <http://whispersinthewind333.blogspot.com>. Hija tieħu gost taqsam ir-rigal tal-kelma ma' oħrajn.

Paul Callus was born in Ħal Safi, Malta. He is married to Sheila née Ackland-Snow and they have two children. He is a retired teacher, and has been active in the literary field for around 50 years. He has published three books, and has had several short stories and poems published in various magazines, anthologies and online sites. His preferred writing mediums are Maltese and English. He is also a proofreader and translator.

Paul Callus twieled Ħal Safi, Malta. Huwa miżżewweġ lil Sheila née Ackland-Snow u għandhom żewġt itfal. Ħadem ta' għalliem, u ilu attiv fil-qasam letterarju għal madwar 50 sena. Ippubblika tliet kotba u kellu għadd ta' poeżiji u stejjer qosra li dehru f'gazzetti, antoloġiji u siti online. Jippreferi jikteb l-aktar bil-Malti u bl-Ingliż. Huwa wkoll proofreader u traduttur.

At the Jingu Altar

Karla Linn Merrifield

At the Shinto shrine,
bow twice, clap twice, bow again,
make a little wish:
mine that this kiss will find you,
tasting of spring's first apple.

~United States

From Sunrise

Karla Linn Merrifield

My transforming kiss
turns bitterest Sevilla
oranges into
tangy marmalade to coat
your tongue this Spanish morning.

~United States

Counter Attack

Karla Linn Merrifield

Somali pirates
kidnapped this kiss, but barely—
I swash-buckled through
their throngs armed solely with love,
my kiss rescued, delivered.

~United States

Out of Arabia

Karla Linn Merrifield

There once was a kiss from Dubai
that was swept away far and high.
In a storm of sand,
by Allah's great hand,
it came to you, a holy sigh.

~United States

From China Beach

Karla Linn Merrifield

By dawn's early light,
this historic kiss escapes
Vietnam disguised
as one dragonfly among
their buzzing battalion.

~United States

Karla Linn Merrifield, nine-time Pushcart-Prize nominee and National Park Artist-in-Residence, has had 700+ poems appear in dozens of journals and anthologies. She has 14 books to her credit. Following her 2018 Psyche's Scroll (Poetry Box Select) is her full-length book Athabaskan Fractal: Poems of the Far North from Cirque Press. She is a frequent contributor to The Songs of Eretz Poetry Review, and assistant editor and poetry book reviewer emerita for The Centrifugal Eye.

Malta

Kath Abela Wilson

swaying palms
the sea held you
a small island inhabited
by many tribes
your blue veined dawn

in the end a small fountain
paradise by your door
spilling over
I feed the birds all night
while you are leaving

your own homeland
always unreachable
mossback
a turtle as if you carried
another continent on your back

if only we could ask
the unreachable ones
a few questions
we are dimmed by their shadows
and already the waning moon

~Malta, Egypt, and Santa Barbara, California, USA

Kath Abela Wilson

hesitation of a squirrel
as I go by
eye to eye
knowing the ins and outs
of our unspoken desires

~Pasadena, California, USA

cherita

Kath Abela Wilson

my mother
how she wrapped

herself in indigo

waiting
like the sphinx
she was born as

~Port Said, Egypt

Kath Abela Wilson remains true to her dismay at what has come of the ideals and dreams wishes and strong stances taken by those who wish kindness to be the basis for our communities and nations. Her Maltese mother, Mary Abela, a peacemaker, and strong to the end at 95, continues to inspire her. She is the author of The Owl Still Asking, Tanka for Troubled Times, Locofo Chaps, Chicago, 2017, available from Lulu, and Figures of Humor and Strange Beauty, her free verse odyssey that ends with a cherita, available from Amazon and from the publisher, Glass Lyre Press, Chicago, 2019. She lives with her mathematician flute collector and player Rick Wilson in Pasadena, and Santa Barbara, California.

Cherita

Keitha Keyes

believing

the only good one
is a dead one

I whack the spider
and watch
its death curl

which words

will I add
to this sympathy card . . .

his widow
must not learn
how much he meant to me

~Sydney, NSW, Australia

Keitha Keyes

fleeing
from domestic violence
I leave
all my belongings
taking only the children

as he reaches
the skies of Australia
Santa replaces
his red and white suit
with shorts and thongs

born
the wrong colour
my neighbour
seeks a fair go
in this white world

~Sydney, NSW, Australia

In Passing

Keitha Keyes

As a child I quite liked going to church.

One of my old aunts used to sing really loudly for a little while, have a rest, and then break into song again. That was funny.

And I thought the Holy Communion thing was interesting. With the adults lining up at the altar for a sip of something out of a silver cup and something to eat. I wanted to do that, too, when I was old enough.

But the best part was watching the collection plate go around. The adults usually put notes on the plate and the children plonked down their coins. I used to sit at the end of a row of seats so that I could pass the plate on to the next row. That way I had longer to look at all the money. And think about how rich the minister must be. And wonder what he'd spend the money on.

    why do we recall
    some bits and pieces
    of our childhood
    and not others . . .
    unfinished jigsaws

~Sydney, NSW, Australia

Keitha Keyes lives in Sydney, in a small house decorated with ship models, antique irons and trivets. And a cocker spaniel. Her retirement would be very empty without the lure of writing tanka, haiku, senryu, cherita and other poetry.

Kira Nash

tiny tyrannosaur
waltzing in the sink
watching him float
i almost can't hear
the noise of everything

another country
i'm not sure anymore
what language i speak
at least they have
bio pink pancakes

wooden ikea chair
soft cotton blanket
the cat and a toy lion
in this little corner
i'm home again

it's like a church
with stained glass windows
a high wooden ceiling
at least we can sleep
in nurtured peace

field mice and flowers
glowing autumn gold
now i remember
i left the door open
for a day like today

sleepy face nuzzles
into my arm
this greatest blessing
quietly purring
the world better

why is it that feet
get so very cold
i wonder if they're lonely
so far away
from the heart

i get lost
every evening
but most nights
gracious sleep
guides me home to morning

sea winds tear across
eucalyptus hills
are they blowing away
the past five months
or trying to shake us free

so grateful for bedtime
even when pain
keeps me awake
at least at night
it's ok to be tired

~*Portugal*

Kira Nash lives in France for the second time and hopes that she'll soon be able to root herself. She finds joy in cups of tea with her husband and cuddles with her cat; she loves gardening and being in the water. The human world bewilders her, but flowers, starlight, and sunshine sing her soul to peace. Kira works as a writer, editor, artist, and teacher, and can be found at www.kiakari.com.

these autumn nights

Liam Wilkinson & *Joy McCall*

sitting alone beside the road
beneath the white September moon
a doll made from corn and crocus
turns to watch as I pass

she whispers 'I am beautiful'
forgetting the Spirit hears all
and in a flash her sight is lost
the road grows cold and dark

from the blackness, a long low growl
I kneel to take the doll in hand
fearful of the red-eyed Rye Wolf
that haunts these autumn nights

~North Yorkshire, England / *Norwich, England*

Liam Wilkinson lives in North Yorkshire, England. He is the author of Seeing Double: Tanka Pairs (Skylark, 2016) and co-author of Singing into Darkness: Tanka and Ryuka Triptychs (Wildflower Poetry Press, 2017) and Is it the Wind That Howls? Ryuka Triptychs (Skylark, 2018) with Joy McCall.

Joy McCall has written tanka most of her life and published many books. Lately, because of reading Liam's poetry, she also loves.

Lorne Henry

inch by inch
I move the furniture
to the shed
I'll need to borrow
muscles for the tools

new pink moon
lies on its back
Scorpio
watches over her
tail poised ready

our new home
streetlights light the way
no need
for a torch at night
my dog's new kingdom

so much dust
from the old farmhouse
piece by piece
a damp cloth reveals
the original

mandarins
globes of hollowed skin
hang from the tree
a rainbow lorikeet
takes a segment from my hand

the rattle
of sliding windows
a sound
that's part of my new home
a puzzle for my dog

evening
flocks of galahs
fly to roost
headed for the hills
from who knows where

~*Manning Valley, NSW, Australia*

Lorne Henry has been writing tanka for many years and lives in the Manning Valley in NSW Australia. The new home provides different soundscapes and views and a different way of life.

M. Kei

making my morbid rounds
from web site to web site
during the pandemic
looking up statistics

the dead
      the dying
            the unknown

~United States

M. Kei is a tall ship sailor and award-winning poet who lives on Maryland's Eastern Shore. He is the editor of the journal, Atlas Poetica: A Journal of World Tanka, and the anthology, Stacking Stones, An Anthology of Short Tanka Sequences. His most recent collection of poetry is January, A Tanka Diary. He can be followed on Twitter @kujakupoet, or visit AtlasPoetica.org.

Mark Jun Poulos

off to my therapist's office
summer sun oven-like
broiling face, eyes—
stutter-stutter of pounding drills
reek of fresh urine everywhere

eyeing me
a pretty Korean girl smiles—
scar on her chest
resembling lips
touched with a hint of rouge

~Los Angeles, California, USA

Asemic* Tanka

M. Kei

tutuavula tu
a tetwe ula ovay
atu vala wey
tutuvanwe etwu nahd
daemwin evay oteyn nohd

~Chesahwinwey

* *Asemic writing is generally considered to be a wordless form of writing with no semantic content. I decided to apply it to tanka.*

M. Kei inwah o maluwin katey-a nohm atme somahdaemunk.

Sedoka

Mark Jun Poulos

downtown sun
glaring off my glasses
I head to my therapist's—
sound of a pile driver
pounding into asphalt
echoing the turmoil in my head

outside a Catholic school
a Virgin Mary statue
spotlessly white, gracefully carved—
a homeless man
bearded, gaunt, sun-darkened
lays flowers on her shoulders

in bumper-to-bumper
L.A. traffic
honking relentlessly
at the driver in front—
on his baby-on-board sticker
image of an AK-47

seated alone
at a park bench
a stout black woman—
glossy, smooth, ebony complexion
tinged a faint blue
in sunlight filtering through a tree

pulling into a space
at a McDonald's
headlights beaming into
a tall hedge in front—
that shudders like a great beast
as a horde of rats scurry through it in terror

walking home
delighted to see
in the darkness of an autumn night
a moth fluttering past my knees
a tiny scrap of confetti
blowing whitely in warm dry wind

perched atop a Mormon temple's massive wall
a line of ravens
face the western sky—
eyes glowing like rubies
as they stare into
the setting sun

fearless, oblivious to my presence
that big raven
down there beside me—
treading pine needles
strewn over the sidewalk
with soft, quiet steps

walking past an autoshop
I pause entranced—
gazing down at shadows
cast by palm fronds
swaying softly on sea breezes
like giant feather fans

~*Los Angeles, California, USA*

more tanka about Ron

Mark Jun Poulos

heavy rains
Ron's nowhere to be seen—
yesterday's breadcrumbs
lie scattered by a lamppost
mushy, wet

the rain lifts—
Ron's outside
seated at the foot of my window
tearing up white bread
for the happy pigeons

desiccated
that's what it is
he said when a woman
complimented him
on his clean-shaven face

turning it round
Ron gazes into a small crystal tree
a Christmas gift—
illumined from within
by a green bulb

~Los Angeles, California, USA

Mark Jun Poulos is from L.A. He loves nature, Japan's countryside and Tu Fu. He wishes he could travel throughout the U.S. and the world more often. He hopes that by steeping his mind in Asian Classical poetry—Chinese, Korean and Japanese—he can learn how to write good tanka. He currently works at a grocery store.

Marshall Bood

they hold nothing
I have done wrong
against me . . .
I rattle
a cup of ice

my daily battle
waiting for medication time,
then waiting for them
to kick in . .
icy sidewalks

no longer bothering
to cover up
the graffiti
on the abandoned building . . .
autumn rain

~Regina, Saskatchewan, Canada

Marshall Bood lives and works in Regina, Saskatchewan, Canada. He has a chapbook forthcoming with Ugly Duckling Press in 2021. His poetry has recently appeared in Presence, bottle rockets, The Heron's Nest and others.

With a Red Knapsack
a tanka rensaku

Matsukaze

sputtering candle: another day of an unmade bed and these juvenile thoughts about nothing

stayed in bed all day-didn't get up and out until after 3 pm what journey am i on in life

local bus passing some kid with a red knapsack i on the balcony taking it all in

on the balcony taking in the day heat people and sounds—i've developed this smoking habit

beautiful hydrangeas and a few bougainvillea i am still a grown man missing his mother

police sirens outside bagging up trash i decide i can't continue this depressive funk any longer

aiming to read this book on mindfulness i even decide to set up a voice lesson with maestro

i have been grossly unhappy. i have been bitter. my perception is wounded and a bit toxic

no more patience for much of anything tonight i thumb restlessly through the Man'yoshu

what am i looking for exactly? news of a traffic pile up my thoughts bumper to bumper too

for a moment i want to hide in the belly of a forest of black pines . . . my life's music is Mahler

i want to look at life through the eyes of a sunflower just now i can't shake this blues

these black curtains: sentinels that keep moonlight and sunspill out of my space

in this time of life sticking with making tanka in one line one breath of feeling

my sangria candle is almost done burning-the young ones' in the living room watching anime

even in my grief still finding time to be a help to others *Baba who will help me shake this pain
    (*Baba means 'honored father' in some African and Mid Eastern languages/my term of endearment for God)

i am not Mokichi Takuboku Ryokan Saigyo Kawana Tawara Goldstein or Kei i'm becoming me everyday

red lights, yes red lights . . . the ones Mokichi spoke of i find myself searching for them everywhere

'in my childhood' beginning of one of Aya's tanka, there are things i can't recall in my childhood unsure of the direction my bedroom window faces-mama i really don't know how to continue

every night i go to bed to albums of Shakespearean tragedies: 'Macbeth,' 'King Lear,' and 'Julius Caesar'

october in a few weeks my birthday in a few weeks i am an october child a man of the blues

huge clouds piling up at the bottom of the sky appears a thunderstorm is soon to arrive

didn't leave my apartment today-the day darkened and lightened as my mood dictated

tonight when i should be in bed still awake watching "Mannix" and making tanka

revisiting honkadori and the borrowing of phrases from other people's tanka when my words are few

damp sleeves and this summer heat no Princess Shikishi i do not have the time to romanticize life

urban rainpour: we sit in his parked car talking about yesterday and the possible future

i am a libra this capacity for trauma and pain has rapidly lost all its elasticity

where i live there is no days of falling snow only these internal tears for the loss of mama

Baba it has been difficult praying much less studying Torah-i cannot locate any of my drive

all this talk of tanka lineation and syllables i simply count words 10–20 and sing in one line

this very air tanka slices of life feeling and all things holding yesterday now and tomorrow

is it time for another book am i more mature and settled after mother's death and getting shot

does tragedy settle a person with metal fingernails i scratch at an iron heaven

noticing the upside down penny on the ground wonder what it's thinking and what its world is like

is it even possible for a person to kill a memory there are so many i have tried to ignore . . . but they're still there

the inside man seated in a corner wearing shadows and a bit o neglect . . . now is the time to rescue me

with a red knapsack now and then leaning to stare into the wide mouth of life of this world

most times feeling like i'm not really living i plant a white chrysanthemum in the hair of my dead life

everyone in my home asleep i push sleep away in order to read a collection of zuihitsu this year a harvest of death . . . in two weeks Rosh Hashanah will come-can i embrace the newness

these tanka are origami i fold and bend them into . . . is it pretty shapes or reality

~Dallas, Texas, USA

A Bit of Cilantro

Matsukaze

didn't know the air turned damp, or even cooler; i wait for a rainpour that doesn't come

nearly 10 pm, still my replacement hasn't arrived; feel an urge to write a zuihitsu

i want hands on my face by a love i've never known…Genji is born; his mother dies

Genji's given to his grandmother, he's closer to his father; the emperor at this time

now that mama is gone, who will nurse me? my only grandmother is a recluse

haven't seen my father's mother in over 10 years, a man waking through the dark

"i love myself" my mantra in the days to come until it sinks in becoming real

from where i stand, seeing neon lights in the distance; this city is very tired

trying this 'love myself' thing out. he said he's on the way to pick me up

told myself a few years back i was a black Genji: seems i'm everyone but myself

a bit of cilantro in these beans, while they simmer i ponder the fullness of existence

in this Genji world, out of touch with reality, unfamiliar with the world in me

~Dallas, Texas, USA

*Matsukaze from Dallas, Texas
a written, visual, vocal storyteller.
he enjoys the immediacy of
short form poetry and their ability
to document and archive life.*

In a World of Hurt

Michael H. Lester

where have you been
my dissipated
wayward child
those wild eyes unblinking
those lips so strangely curled

thinner now
sullen and forlorn
you set off
to seek your fortune
on the day you were born

stay awhile
your room is just the same
we kept your books
your sheets of poetry
and your calligraphy

we wiped away
the gathering dust
every morning
we opened wide the curtains
and closed them each night

tell me
where have you been
my wayward child
those wild eyes unblinking
those lips so strangely curled

A Rolling Thunder Revue: A Bob Dylan Story A Hard Rain's Gonna Fall

~Los Angeles, California, USA

Has it Finally Come to This?

Michael H. Lester

as I lay dying
hardly able to lift an arm
I shed a tear
for the poor mosquito
supping this anemic blood

I pity the spider
that prances about my neck
spinning its web
as if I were the easel
for its next masterpiece

the cricket
scampering about the floor
chirping gaily
brings a certain comfort
to these heavy eyelids

the dust
gathering on the window
thickens with passing days
and still, no one comes
to change these soiled sheets

no one to tell
how it feels to die alone
forgotten
slowly wasting away—
being eaten alive

~Los Angeles, California, USA

Michael H. Lester

while lying in bed
wishing to fall asleep
strange thoughts
crop up out of nowhere
like mushrooms in the night

and the King
having seen his reflection
in a looking glass
that cannot tell a lie
calls for his own impeachment

an old photo
of my ex-wife and me
wearing a hat
I barely remember her
but I'll never forget the hat

generations
are like ocean waves
one after the other
they fall upon the shore
and then they are gone

tall in the saddle
the most beautiful girl
I've ever seen
and just like that
she's gone

the crumbling
of the American dream
rests in the hands
of cowards and bigots
the color of curdled milk

sleep will not come
this hail-drumming night
for I have left
my begging bowl
in a tangle of grass

at the convention
we exchange meaningful looks
she hands me her card
you never know when you might need
a marriage counselor

crouched
under a sea of umbrellas
urchins
pick tourists' pockets
at the rainbow's end

for the first time
I realize the same word—
asylum
is not just for the insane
but also for the persecuted

*have you had sex
with multiple partners?*
counting sheep
I am finally able
to fall asleep

should I disappear
like some ancient monolith
rest assured
I will not be back
for I never did exist

an autumn leaf
clings fast to the beech
will it take
a frigid winter wind
to bring it to its knees?

twenty percent
of the world's oxygen
up in smoke
when will it be possible
to breathe a sigh of relief?

I can still hear
my mother's fingers
tap, tap, tapping
as I shudder at the sound
of dirt pounding her coffin

her mother
still spry at ninety-nine
scuttles down the walk
clicking and clacking
like a loose-limbed marionette

she lives downriver
past the Kern County line
where the catfish jump
I seen her there sometimes
but she don't notice me

on these old shoulders
each raindrop feels the same
but the touch
of your comforting hand
is unlike any other

~Los Angeles, California, USA

A Bumper Crop

Michael H. Lester

no sour grapes, though
the grapefruit seeds I planted
have grown strong
the two that survived
the ransacking of a stranger

bushy and dark green
they seem oblivious
to the clover
growing ever bolder
to the point of indecency

inexplicably
the occasional worm
lay desiccated
on the concrete driveway
where the dog soaks up sun

this year
the tomato plants thrive—
one upside
to the catastrophe
of global warming

as a bonus
even the jalapeño plants
have fruited
I am a veritable
cultivator supreme!

~the backyard of a modest home on Los Angeles, California, USA

Where do Poems Come From and Where do They Go?

Michael H. Lester

    it is not so easy
    to write a certain kind
    of poem
    as it is to let the poem
    write itself

I think about how to get known in the tanka world, and winning contests seems to be one way. Shiki found fame with haiku early in his career in part by entering contests. It is a tradition in waka, too, going back all the way.

I soon realize the surest way to fame is to write a lot of good poetry.

It also helps to have a tireless booster, a wise mentor, and an unerring guide in the treacherous tanka jungle.

    how tall he's grown
    with a mother's love
    but now she's gone
    how pale and wan
    and where is the moon tonight?

    ~Los Angeles, California, USA

In the Early Morning Rain

Michael H. Lester

On the bus ride to work, rain or shine, there is always the same man stumbling up and down the aisle raving about the end of days, complaining that no one ever listens.

One day, he mumbles, *one day, you will say "Sam was right. Sam was right."*

    crapulous
    he slurs his words
    remonstrating
    over some perceived slight
    to anyone who will listen

The man in the seat next to me folds his newspaper into quarters to read an article on the sports page about some rookie on the Detroit Tigers baseball team named Al Kaline.

    I learn
    on a bus ride to work
    the technique
    for reading a newspaper
    in a cramped space

The bus stops one block from my office building in downtown Detroit. Sam and I get off at the same exit. He takes shelter under my umbrella, nudging me off to one side. I nudge him halfway back so each of us has a shoulder in the rain. *How are you doing, Sam?* I inquire. *Who's Sam?* he asks.

    ~Detroit, Michigan, USA

Not Yet Out of the Woods

Michael H. Lester

As a young teen, a friend and I lure a neighbor boy into the woods, tie him to a tree, and leave him there for the wolves. Next day, his older brother approaches me from behind on my way to school, and without warning, pushes me down to the ground. I deserve worse, I suppose.

if you do harm
a lifetime of bad karma
may soon follow
in the clever guise
of an older brother

~*Meyer's woods and the mean streets of Detroit, Michigan, USA*

Michael H. Lester is a CPA and attorney living in Los Angeles, California. Passionate about short-form poetry, Michael's poetry has been widely published in prestigious poetry journals and has won numerous awards. Michael has recently authored and self-published an illustrated children's book, Cassandra and the Strange Tale of the Blue-Footed Boobies, and a book of poetry, Notes from a Commode - Volume I, both available on Amazon.com. You can reach Michael at mhlester@ca.rr.com and twitter: @mhlester.

Michael O'Brien

in a dark morning
making your way
to a day of labour
you and the moon
moving towards death

you notice
a sea of trash
you become a fish hook
jumping in
and nothing else

bullet holes
the size of cranberries
time
as always indifferent

beaujolais nouveau
somehow
this late in autumn
knee deep
in wild strawberries

feeling nothing
about anything
breaking down
in the rain
horse shit

~*Helsinki, Finland*

Michael O'Brien is the author of numerous collection the most recent being Silent Age (Alien Buddha Press). His writing has been published widely in print and on the internet and translated into other languages. He is also the curator of Weird Laburnum. You can follow him on twitter @michaelobrien22.

The Fish

N. Nyberg

Water
slips from silver scales,
gills still working in the dry air,
a single, unblinking eye staring silently
into space.

~Red Lake, Minnesota, USA

Alphabet Soup

N. Nyberg

My
breath puts momentary
creases in the soup spoon's
tiny, literary
pool.

~Lunch, with toddlers, Rapid City, South Dakota, USA

N. Nyberg

Feeling
old injuries that have calcified,
I limp from my bedroom
into the kitchen,
to coffee, sunlight, and the day's events.

Melons—
poised in their pregnant, still-life arrangements
here in the garden, this late-summer
morning.

The
bathroom faucet drips steadily,
keeping perfect time with the rhythm
of a quiet day.

~Mountain View, California, USA

N. Nyberg was raised in mostly rural Minnesota in the 1960s, has since lived for extended periods in a variety of places, including Iowa City, Iowa, the Bay Area of northern California, New York City, and Los Angeles, and now divides his time between Minneapolis, Minnesota, and Rapid City, South Dakota. Over the years, he has practiced law and taught, mostly law and philosophy, raised a family, and lived a life.

Nathalie Lauro

Nathalie Lauro, English-French Translator

Nathalie Lauro, traductrice anglaise-française

the dark
November rains
are always
cruel
for lovers

les pluies sombres
de novembre
sont toujours
cruelles
pour les amoureux

I trust
the hills and
the moons . . .
it is simple
You?

je crois
les collines et
les lunes . . .
c´est simple
toi?

I listen to
the misty skies
they talk
about you
sometimes

j´écoute
les ciels brumeux
ils parlent
de toi
parfois

blue moon
reflexions
on the waves
I'm a bit
lost

réflexions
de la lune bleue
sur les vagues
je suis un peu
perdue

some jazz notes
under my skin
you are
far away
now

quelques notes de jazz
sous la peau
tu es
loin
à présent

in the fresh mud
you will
find
my
answers

dans la boue fraîche
tu
trouveras
mes
réponses

feel the springtime
in the branches
the pink blossoms
smile
to you

sens
le printemps
dans les branches
les fleurs roses
te sourient

midnight
is waiting
for us
I'm alone
in the darkness

minuit
nous attend
je suis
seule
dans l'obscurité

the tea leaves
infuse
they will show
the right way
soon

les feuilles de thé
infusent
elles montreront
le bon chemin
bientôt

I feel
the pain
among the souls
let's give them
rainbows

je sens
la douleur
parmi les âmes
donnons leur
des arcs-en-ciel

~Cap d'Ail, France

Nathalie Lauro was born in Marseille in 1965 and lives on the French Riviera since 1983. She obtained a Master's degree in Management and made a career in Palaces of the Riviera. Today, oriented in another direction, she shares her life between art, literary, poetry . . .
- *Poetry published in french magazines*
- *Tankas published in Cirrus Tankas*
- *A collection "Vides et Sensations"*
- *A novel "Une méditerrannéenne à Hanovre"*

Nathalie Lauro est née à Marseille en 1965 et vit sur la Côte d'Azur depuis 1983. Elle a obtenu un Master en Management et fait une carrière dans les Palaces de la Riviera. A présent, orientée dans une toute autre direction, elle partage sa vie entre art, littérature, et poésie . . .
- *Poésie publiée dans de nombreuses revues françaises*
- *Tankas publiés dans la revue francophone Cirrus Tankas*
- *Un recueil de poésie " Vides et Sensations"*
- *Un roman "Une méditerranéenne à Hanovre"*

Serenity

Neal Whitman

This morning my wife went to Whole Foods where she was shopping in the herbal tea aisle. She returned home with this tale. As Elaine reached for a box of Yogi Calming (Helps Soothe Mild Tension) Tea, a woman, maybe in her 40s, queried in a gruff voice: "Do you know how to bake bread?" Elaine responded gently, "No, I'm sorry. It's been years." "Well," the woman spurted, "I'm asking every white-haired woman I see."

Elaine, by the way, has just turned 72. Her hair has turned a soft, natural grey. She espied her inquisitor pounce on a woman with snow-white hair making her way down the aisle, "Do you know how to bake bread? I'm asking every…"

    this afternoon
    she sits cross-legged
    hands on her knees
    she breathes in and out
    holding her "disposition"

~Pacific Grove, California, USA

Neal Whitman lives in Pacific Grove, California, with his wife, Elaine, where they find serenity and calmness. After all, if you are lucky enough to live by the ocean, then you are lucky enough. The people and place of the Monterey Peninsula inspire the creativity in both of them.

Patricia Prime

the soft beret
perched on his bald head
in the photograph
he sent me many years ago
when we first became friends

~New Zealand

Morning Glory

Patricia Prime

. . . cast adrift by a faint ripple of heron's wings, the sudden birth of bird song flutters across the river. I know a language lost to me lies there, clear as the blue morning glory open to the thrill of thunder clattering and the lightening in my soul. I'm walking in the Japanese garden. A man stands quite still, observing me with his brown eyes, then he wanders off to examine a haiku engraved on a rock. There is traffic noise in the distance. Willow branches stream in the breeze. I measure my steps: Japanese wooden bridge over the river, river to rock garden, rock garden to hill-climb, hill-climb to road, the road back home.

    end of summer
    blue morning glory
    trumpets in the garden
    where doves fly
    to and from the dove-cote

~New Zealand

Peaceful Protest

Patricia Prime

New Zealand pioneered
peaceful protest in the 1860s
when the settlement at Parihaka
became a symbol of non-violence
to colonial confiscation of land

in March of 1930
Gandhi invented the form
of nonviolent resistance
when he led a crowd across India
to make salt from sea water

Mahatma Gandhi
the founder of passive resistance
was assassinated
by a Hindu fanatic
who detested his calls for peace

in Tiananmen Square
a mysterious man
stood alone in front
of a line of tanks to protest
at the slow pace of promised reform

after the massacre
of Muslims in New Zealand
many women
chose to wear the hijab
as a sign of protest

~New Zealand

Patricia was born in the UK and has lived in NZ for 40 years. She was an early education teacher for 35 years. She currently has a collection of poems with an Indian editor and is looking forward to a book being released this year. The editor also interviewed Patricia for a magazine article late last year, which has been published in an Indian journal. Patricia is the co-editor of Kokako, reviews/interviews editor of Haibun Today, reviewer for Takahe and writes reviews for several journals.

Or So It Seems: A Tanka Sequence

Ray Spitzenberger

snap of finger
decades seem like a second
"husband and wife"
pronounced by her dear pastor
"In sickness and in health"

three careers
with beginnings and endings
the good life
first kids and grandkids, and then
cardio and uro docs

bp gauge
on end-table north of couch
another
on end-table south of couch
one for her and one for me

oh so short
our life is just a brief burp
but also
it is a hot fudge sundae,
short and sweet, or so it seems

~United States

Ray Spitzenberger has published in numerous publications, including Atlas Poetica (Tanka), Better than Starbucks (Haiku), Chrysanthemum (Haiku), Red River Review (Free Verse), Tanka Journal (Tanka), Grit (feature), Handbook of Texas (history), just to name a few. My light-hearted book, It Must Be the Noodles, is on sale at Amazon.com, and my book of poems, Open Prairies, will be out this summer. You can read more about me at: https://rayspitzenberger.com.

Rp Verlaine

children in cages
is now the norm
the highlight of their day
standing in cramped halls
while the rooms are cleaned

in luminescent light
I lose all awe of stars
when her shadow emerges
coming close enough
to touch mine

I watch her sleep
each gentle breath
new ocean waves
pulling me close to
drown quicker

she asks you to stay
afraid of being alone
with ghosts of the past
that circle a future
already haunted by ghosts

she pulls me to her warmth
where she says other men
lingered like thieves
gave love like illusionists
then left quiet as winter

~New York, USA

Rp Verlaine lives and writes in New York City. He has an MFA in creative writing from City College. He taught in New York Public schools for many years. His poetry has appeared in Atlas Poetica, The Linnet's Wings, Haikuniverse, Stardust Haiku, The Local Train, Proletaria, Scryptic, Humankind Journal, Fractured Haiku, Under The Basho, Plum Tree Tavern, Fresh Out Magazine, Ugly Writers, Prune Juice, Incense Dreams, Best Poetry, Blazevox, Pikers Press, Bleached-Butterfly, Poems 'bout Love & Hate anthology.

Sandra Renew

relief at last
first downpour for years
rain gauge brims
every waterway running—
just wet earth or scent of hope?

months of false forecasts
at last the clouds deliver
stalks and stems unfold
we check maps, predictions
greedy for more

one day we're wilting
in 40 degree heat
stifling smoke haze,
then overnight the deluge—
we complain about raincoats

even in the rain
curlews and currawongs
are busy
humans cry about the drought
complain about the Wet

in drought-breaking rain
the bush changes colour
smells rich and alive
wet kangaroos chew new shoots—
just add water

~Canberra, Australia

Sandra Renew's poetry is published in Griffith Review (forthcoming), The Blue Nib, Canberra Times, Contemporary Haibun Online, Hecate, Axon, Australian Poetry Journal 2019, Shuffle: An Anthology of Microlit, (Spineless Wonders, 2019). Her recent collections are Acting Like a Girl, Recent Work Press, 2019 and The Orlando Files, Ginninderra Press, 2018. Sandra lives and writes in Canberra, Australia.

Scott Moss

this lugubrious mutt
outside the coffee shop window
gives off a marathon
yawn, and i copy
him out of solidarity

an orange volkswagon
bus sputters through the crossroads,
scattering amber leaves.
each settles back in a new place,
into another stillness

in the town where i
grew up, the hills, the streets, my
elementary school,
here in my hometown, an adult,
i long for home.

65 on 5,
square framed by rusty metal
hangs the fell sullen
partial face and blinking eye
of a confined youngling colt

wide overcast
charcoal hints of a distant fire
this path like clay
the union pacific will storm past soon,
tweaking the daisies

from london brown study
thick fogged its way to
manhattan, now blue funk
basement hovel, wet window pain,
a trumpet whimpering

a dilapidated
outbuilding squats short in
desolate farmland.
the wind within blows pages
of a phonebook back and forth

the ducks don't know they
live here in boise. they don't
know they're american
they don't have driver licenses
they live by this single river

the moss grows
on the surface of a rock
it has never once
thought that it has never
been to santiago, chile

cresting the last hill
of my journey
to this dubious
destination, and i see
clearly, a seaside graveyard.

~Montana, USA

Scott Moss is currently working on an MFA in poetry in Missoula, Montana, USA. He writes both Japanese-style poems as well as more traditional western-style poems.

Sterling Warner

Harpoon horizons
watch whaling apparitions
glide to Nantucket;
oil drums filled, scrimshaw pipes lit,
sailors dream of Rapunzel.

Capitola beach
shells, kelp, jiggers commingle
toes dig deep wet sand;
damp August t-shirts cling to
young lovers playing at dusk.

Twilight forms merging
like harpsichord concertos
escape fall dust, winter winds
physical young girls and boys
become one like their elders.

~Washington, USA

An author, poet, and educator, Sterling Warner's works have appeared in dozens of literary magazines, journals, and anthologies such as In the Grove, The Flatbush Review, Leaf by Leaf, Street Lit: Representing the Urban Landscape, American Mustard, the Atherton Review, and Metamorphoses. Warner's has written five volumes of poetry: Rags and Feathers, Without Wheels, ShadowCat, Edges, and Memento Mori. Currently, he lives in Union, WA and is working on a flash fiction collection.

Tanja Trček

Tanja Trček, Slovenian-English Translator

Angleško-slovenski prevod: Tanja Trček

In a silver frame
of the night
her midnight face
vanishes
into silence

V srebrnem okvirju
noči
se njen polnočni obraz
razblini
v tišino

A rain of memories—
come!
let's splash
through puddles
past

Dež spominov
pridi!
greva čofotat
po lužah
preteklosti

Within
a raindrop
she falls
silently
at midnight

Ona —
v dežni kapljici
pade
tiho
ob polnoči

The blossom
opens
slowly
slowly
deepening the silence

Cvet
se odpre
počasi
počasi
poglobi tišino

A sweet blush
of flowers' breath
drifts above
the gently flowing
river

Sladka rdečica
rožnega diha
polzi nad
nežnim tokom
reke

Summer flowers
long wilted
but their fragrance
still floats
in this autumn world

Cvetje poletja
odcvetelo dolgo tega
a njihov vonj
še zdaj lebdi
skozi ta jesenski svet

~Golnik, Slovenia / Golnik, Slovenija

Once an all-around athlete, Tanja Trček is now bedbound. She often finds the enormity of her illness overwhelming and seeks refuge in small things, her very favorite among them being tanka. Seemingly small poems, but with the power to give meaning to one's life, maybe to even save lives.

Tanja Trček je bila včasih vsestranska športnica, sedaj pa je vezana na posteljo. Velikokrat je vseobsežnost njene bolezni neznosna, tako da se zateka k drobnim stvarem, med katerimi pa so ji najljubše tanke. Navidezno majcene pesmi, a z močjo, da podarijo življenju smisel, morda celo, da ga rešijo.

Ìtunmọ̀ Àwọn Ẹyẹ
(títèlé Michele Harvey)

Táófìkì Ayéyẹmí

Táófìkì Ayéyẹmí, Onítumọ̀ Yorùbá-Gòr

ẹyẹ méjì
n dúró láìmira lójú òrun . . .
rírántí
ìtunmọ̀ tí eleyì jẹ́
mo pàdánù wọn

funfun àti dúdú
àwọn ìyẹ́ tí n fẹ́ nínú afẹ́fẹ́ . . .
mo ṣi ònkà
wíwọn ìkọ̀kan wọn
lórí ìwọ̀n ìmọ̀ àṣírí

àdán àti òwìwí
jẹ́ ónjẹ lórí tábìlì mi tẹ́lẹ̀
àfìgbà
tí aṣíwájú ìmọ̀ àṣírí mi
ṣímí ní ìríran inú . . .

èwọ̀
ni kí èyán jẹ igún . . .
ṣùgbọ́n aṣájú
sọ wípé onímọ̀ àṣírí
ma n ṣe n̄kan àjèjì

òrún
tàn gba inú àwọn ìyẹ́
ẹyẹ—
kódà ayékòtó n tẹríba
fún ọgbọ́n inú húdíhúdà

~Ìyẹsí Ọtà, Ìpínlẹ̀ Ògùn, Naijiria

Táófìkì Ayéyẹmí, agbẹjọ́rò ati akọwe ọmọ orílẹ̀ èdè Nàìjíríà to ni awọn ewì afòyegbẹ́ nínú atẹjade bí Lucent Dreaming, Ethel-zine, the QuillS, Modern Haiku, Akitsu Quarterly, contemporary haibun online... gba Ẹyẹ Ọwọ̀ nínu ifagagbága 2020 Stephen A. DiBiase Poetry Contest, 2019 Morioka International Haiku Contest ati Ipo Kejì ninu 2016 Christopher Okigbo Poetry Prize.

The Augury of Birds
(after Michele Harvey)

Taofeek Ayeyemi

Taofeek Ayeyemi, Yoruba-English Translator

two birds
hanging still in the sky . . .
recalling
the meaning of this
i lost sight of them

white and black
feathers flying in the air . . .
i lost count
measuring each of them
on the scale of mysticism

bats and owls
were food on my table
until
the mystic master
opened my inner sight . . .

taboo
is to eat vulture . . .
but master
says the dervishes
do strange things

the sun
shines through the wings
of a bird—
even the parrots bow
to the wit of the hoopoe

~Iyesi Ota, Ogun State, Nigeria

Taofeek Ayeyemi, a Nigerian lawyer and writer with works appearing or forthcoming in Lucent Dreaming, Ethel-zine, the QuillS, Modern Haiku, Akitsu Quarterly, contemporary haibun online.... won Honorable Mention Prize in 2020 Stephen A. DiBiase Poetry Contest, 2019 Morioka International Haiku Contest and 2nd Prize in 2016 Christopher Okigbo Poetry Prize.

The Stone Rose

Tim Gardener

Back to the wall, you have a view of the street sloping towards the river, where the docked boat, full of dog rose and rot, is marked *private*, first voyage, forgotten. Rain drops from weatherboard cladding fill an open mind, a grey face the perfect complement for charcoal sky and cobble stones. The belt coils around your waist like a serpent, collar framing a fixed smile. This restraint is only threatened by wind funnelling along the lane, rattling attic windows.

a dash of lilac
from the flower
in untended hair . . .
a statue's rose
clutched tight

~*Upnor, Kent, UK*

Emptiness, free refill

Tim Gardiner

A chance to stretch the legs, explore the airport. The lack of a Visa prohibits exploration of Beijing; besides six hours is not really long enough to visit Tiananmen Square or the Forbidden City. I need sleep more than anything else, a few snatched minutes on the flight from Tokyo far from adequate. Stretched out on boarding gate seating, it's impossible to get any meaningful rest, besides thoughts of leaving you are still too raw. Without any yuan, I have only one option for refreshment. Warm water from the free fountain is all I've got . . .

airport
restricted area
a tear cannot
be suppressed
any longer

~*Beijing airport, Beijing, China*

Fire Woman

Tim Gardiner

I retreat to the safety of the bell tower; the gargoyles' sanctuary. Straightened out, an unfamiliar city stretches before me; where are the hunched gallows? Flames consume the spire, smoke lost to the Parisian sky. Clinging to the rope, I notice a figure gliding through the inferno below, the collapsed ceiling, no impediment. The fire doesn't touch her, or the fumes overcome. Her eyes smoulder like ruins.

untouched
rooftop hive . . .
the beekeeper
needs no protection
from my sting

~*Notre Dame, Paris, France*

Dr Tim Gardiner is an ecologist, poet and children's author from Manningtree in Essex, UK. His haiku and tanka have been published in over 100 print and online magazines and he has been widely anthologised. His first collection of haiku, On the Edge, was published by Brambleby Books in 2017, followed by The Flintknapper's Ghost (2018) and The Sky, Taken Away (2019).

remembering the Orkneys

Tim Lenton

the sun blinds me
as I try to read while
lying in bed:
and you remember that night
so very long ago

before we crashed
beside the ancient tomb
we took the short,
short flight across the island
reluctant to come back

things disappear—
the bridges and the road
beside the inn;
the house where you left the key
under the dying plant

the standing stones
that sparkle in the rain
beyond the loch
open doors in the landscape
to death and risky life

I balance here
where the cliff falls away
into my dreams
and do not see the castle
I had been aching for

~Orkney Islands, Scotland

broken arm tanka

Tim Lenton

plaster cast off
I am exposed to wind
sun and water:
my skin flakes and tightens up
too vulnerable now

hairs on my arm
spring to slow attention
out of the blood,
and the scarlet tide ripples
toward my naked wrist

uncommonly tight
those muscles push and pull
against my sleeve:
I challenge gravity but
fall short every time

autumn evenings
welcome my new freedom:
the crisp cold air
opens me up, kisses me
and sets me free again

I cross the stream
and head for the city
remembering
this morning's double rainbow
above the cathedral

~Norwich, England

Tim Lenton is in his 70s and has concentrated on writing poetry since his retirement. He was formerly a journalist and has lived in his birth town—Norwich, UK—for the last 35 years. He has written tanka since being encouraged to do so by Joy McCall, and they have collaborated on two books which also included his photographs.

Dawn

William Altoft

. . .
you . . .
But now we're sep'rate.
You left to teach
outside the capital.

~Bristol, UK

Yasaman Etemadi

I. Departures

8 am — airport
my favorite place to be
eye-bags heavy but
heart is light. I'm pretending
I don't have a return flight.

II. Fantasy

I'm aloft alone
I don't know where I'm headed
it doesn't matter
though. I am a stone skipping
across earth. Unfindable.

III. Return Flight

8 am — airport
it feels like purgatory
a holding cell that
squeezes my impulse to run
please don't make me go back there.

~West Virginia, USA

Together

Zane Parks

    1961. We've just moved to South Carolina and I'm starting 10th grade. Nita's best friend says she likes me. She's cute. I'm interested. Nita's in 9th grade. She's a majorette in the band. So, she wears an outfit like a bathing suit and twirls a baton. Nita rides to games with the band and during games she sits with the band. At school assemblies, we don't have the guts to leave our own friends, much less sit in the middle of the other's friends. At lunch boys and girls never sit at the same table. At church we sit with our families. Suggesting otherwise stirs up a storm. Sitting next to each other just doesn't seem to be in the cards.

    parents let me
    go to the movie
    despite worries
    it might be too risqué
    elvis

~Cape Coral, Florida, USA

Zane lives on the gulf coast of Florida with his wife Bridget and cats, Miss Kitty and Boaz. In between bouts of writers block, he writes haiku, tanka and related forms. He published his books tiny droppings (haiku and tanka) and Journey (haibun) with Lulu.

William Altoft is a writer in and from (and often on) Bristol, a city in the UK. He writes poetry, prose, prosetry, poetrose . . . Along with shorter poetry, he has written longer works, including his first novel, The Floating Harbour. All his work is freely available on his WordPress.

Yasaman Etemadi is a third year graduate student pursuing her Master's of Science in biology at West Virginia University. She lives in Morgantown, West Virginia, and is 25 years old.

Tanka Translation Project : Special Invitation

M. Kei, Editor

I. Introduction

All readers of *Atlas Poetica : A Journal of World Tanka*, know that we welcome tanka in translation in every issue. Over the course of the more than ten years and forty issues, there have been only five issues that lacked any tanka in translation. So far we have published thirty-seven different languages, although sometimes only one tanka in a given language. In an effort to increase the international availability and appreciation of tanka, we are undertaking a special 'Tanka Translation Project' to be published in ATPO 41. That issue will be devoted entirely to tanka in translation. The results will also be published to the website at AtlasPoetica.org.

To jumpstart the issue, we are offering a selection of tanka and invite readers and anyone else to translate any or all of the selections into any language, as many languages as you like. The results will be published in ATPO 41 on a space available basis. Each poet and translator has agreed to a generous 'copyleft' giving permission for these poems and their translations to be reprinted in other educational and non-profit venues. Therefore, if submitting a translation for this project, please use the subject line 'Tanka Translation Project.' Your submission indicates that you agree for your translation to be republished on these terms, without other editors needing to seek your individual permission.

All translators receive a byline and biography, so please to be sure to include them with your submission in each language you are translating. Pseudonyms are acceptable and biographies should be brief (less than 75 words). Remember to translate all material accompanying the poem, such as the author biography, translator byline and biography, citations, and the acknowledgment.

It is perfectly all right if different translators provide translations of the same poem in the same language. Translation is a fine art and comparing different translations can help give a better sense of the original poem. Translations will be published on a space available basis in ATPO 41.

All the poems in the 'Tanka Translation Project' originally appeared in *Take Five : Best Contemporary Tanka*, volumes 2 through 4. The first three volumes are available at AtlasPoetica.org in the 'Read Tanka' section. Volume 4 is available for purchase at the various Amazon websites around the world, or via special order from your local bookstore. We thank the poets for granting permission for their poems to be used for this project.

When submitting tanka translations, remember not only to provide the translator byline, but to translate the translator byline, all biographies, the previous publication credit. Those who wish to reprint poems and translations must include acknowledgment. Suggested statement:

> "Copyright by the respective authors and translators. Reprinted with permission as part of the 'Tanka Translation Project' published by *Atlas Poetica : A Journal of World Tanka*, No. 41, Autumn, 2020. See ATPO 41 for full details. <AtlasPoetica.org>"

II. Sample Translations

To help you in formatting your translations, we are providing a translation of Ingrid Kunschke's tanka in English, Dutch, and German as an example. (We welcome additional translations of this and all poems.) We offer two formats as suggestions, depending on whether you will be publishing only a single language version, or if you will be offering two or more languages.

If publishing in only one language, we suggest presenting the tanka with its author, translator, the tanka in the language you are providing, the citation, and the biographies as in A below. If providing translations in two or more languages, we suggest presenting them as in B below. Following a standard format will make it easier for us to manage this complex project.

Original:

Ingrid Kunschke

sound asleep
in the Mongol steppe:
nomads
dreaming of cattle
and horses, horses

Previously appeared in Take Five : Best Contemporary Tanka, Volume 3.

Ingrid Kunschke was born in the Netherlands and lives in Minden, Germany. She writes tanka and tanka prose in German, English and Dutch. In 2004 she launched TankaNetz, the first German website to focus on these genres.

Copyright by the respective authors and translators. Reprinted with permission as part of the 'Tanka Translation Project' published by *Atlas Poetica : A Journal of World Tanka*, No. 41, Autumn, 2020. See ATPO 41 for full details. <AtlasPoetica.org>

If you would like to translate a poem, please include a copy of the original with your translation. If translating into one other language, follow the example in A or B below.

Sample Translation A:

Ingrid Kunschke

Ingrid Kunschke, Nederlandse vertaling

in de diepe slaap
van de Mongoolse steppe:
nomaden
dromend van hun vee
en paarden, paarden

Zuvor erschienen in Take Five : Best Contemporary Tanka, Teil 3.

Ingrid Kunschke wurde in den Niederlanden geboren und wohnt in Minden. Sie schreibt Tanka und Tankaprosa in deutscher, englischer und niederländischer Sprache. 2004 veröffentlichte sie TankaNetz, die erste deutsche Website für diese Genres.

Het auteursrecht ligt bij de respectievelijke auteurs en vertalers. Herdrukt met toestemming als onderdeel van het "Tanka Translation Project" uitgegeven door *Atlas Poetica : A Journal of World Tanka*, Nr. 41, Herfst, 2020. Zie ATPO 41 voor volledige details. <AtlasPoetica.org>

Sample Translation B:

Ingrid Kunschke

Ingrid Kunschke, Nederlandse vertaling

Ingrid Kunschke, deutsche Übersetzung

sound asleep
in the Mongol steppe:
nomads
dreaming of cattle
and horses, horses

in de diepe slaap
van de Mongoolse steppe:
nomaden
dromend van hun vee
en paarden, paarden

im tiefen Schlaf
der mongolischen Steppe:
Nomaden
träumend von der Herde
und Pferden, Pferden

Previously appeared in Take Five : Best Contemporary Tanka, Volume 3.

Zuvor erschienen in Take Five : Best Contemporary Tanka, Teil 3.

Eerder verschenen in Take Five : Best Contemporary Tanka, Deel 3.

Ingrid Kunschke was born in the Netherlands and lives in Minden, Germany. She writes tanka and tanka prose in German, English and Dutch. In 2004 she launched TankaNetz, the first German website to focus on these genres.

Ingrid Kunschke wurde in den Niederlanden geboren und wohnt in Minden. Sie schreibt Tanka und Tankaprosa in deutscher, englischer und niederländischer Sprache. 2004 veröffentlichte sie TankaNetz, die erste deutsche Website für diese Genres

Ingrid Kunschke is geboren in Nederland en woont in Minden, Duitsland. Zij schrijft tanka en tanka proza in het Duits, Engels en Nederlands. In 2004 lanceerde zij TankaNetz, de eerste duitstalige website voor deze genres.

Copyright by the respective authors and translators. Reprinted with permission as part of the 'Tanka Translation Project' published by *Atlas Poetica : A Journal of World Tanka*, No. 41, Autumn, 2020. See ATPO 41 for full details. <AtlasPoetica.org>

Het auteursrecht ligt bij de respectievelijke auteurs en vertalers. Herdrukt met toestemming als onderdeel van het "Tanka Translation Project" uitgegeven door *Atlas Poetica: A Journal of World Tanka*, Nr. 41, Herfst, 2020. Zie ATPO 41 voor volledige details. <AtlasPoetica.org>

Das Urheberrecht liegt bei den jeweiligen Autoren und Übersetzern. Nachdruck mit freundlicher Genehmigung als Teil des „Tanka Translation Project" herausgegeben von AtlasPoetica: A Journal of World Tanka, Nr. 41, Herbst, 2020. Siehe ATPO 41 für sämtliche Details. <AtlasPoetica.org>

The goal is always to make a good presentation so that the meta information (poet, translator, citation, biographies, etc) are logically grouped together with the poem so that they are easy to find. Don't forget to include the 'Tanka Translation Project' acknowledgment. All languages are treated equally; readers in any language should be able to have the same experience with the same information.

III. Tanka for Translation in Alphabetical Order by Poet's First Name

We welcome translations of any and all of the following tanka, tanka sequence, and tanka prose in any language. Editors may republish any or all of these in their own non-profit or educational venues provided they follow the guidelines given above. We thank the poets and translators for their generous participation in this project. Let's work together so that readers of any language can share tanka and related literature.

an'ya

my blood and bone
slipping from darkness
into the light
her small skull as round
as a slavic moon

Previously appeared in Take Five : Best Contemporary Tanka, Volume 3.

an'ya is a world-renowned poetess with more than 150 contest wins, 9 editorships, 13 websites, and 23 books to her credit. She has judged 125+ contests and is the founder of numerous haiku/tanka societies and journals. She has been represented in over 200 various literary publications, and her work has been translated into 95 different language dialects.

Ingrid Kunschke

sound asleep
in the Mongol steppe:
nomads
dreaming of cattle
and horses, horses

Previously appeared in Take Five : Best Contemporary Tanka, Volume 3.

Ingrid Kunschke was born in the Netherlands and lives in Minden, Germany. She writes tanka and tanka prose in German, English and Dutch. In 2004 she launched TankaNetz, the first German website to focus on these genres.

James Tipton

One summer night
I found the perfect woman
but by early morning
most of her
had already left.

Previously appeared in Take Five : Best Contemporary Tanka, Volume 3.

James Tipton, poet and beekeeper (1942–2018), author of ten books of poetry, winner of the Colorado Book Award, was widely anthologized and published in tanka journals. The last 13 years of his life he resided in Chapala, Mexico, where he mentored students and wrote short fiction, tanka, and haiku. His favorite topic was women, their allure, and his carnal desires, which earned him the appellation of "writer of virile tanka," a distinction that would have made him smile.

Johannes S. H. Bjerg

struggling
the old woman with a walker
crossing the icy road
her dog in a small bag
along with groceries

Previously appeared in Take Five : Best Contemporary Tanka, Volume 3.

Johannes S. H. Bjerg: Danish writer and artist who writes in Danish and English simultaneously and mainly haiku and haiku related forms. Editor of Bones - "Journal for short verse" (http://www.bonesjournal.com), and sole editor of "the other bunny - for the other kind of haibun" (http://theotherbunny.wordpress.com) and "One Link Chain" - a blog for solo linked verse and haiku sequences (http://onelinkchain.blogspot.dk/) Has published several books: http://megaga.dk/?page_id=530.

Kala Ramesh

she laments
being old and bent
I see her
as a curved branch
laden with fruit

Previously appeared in Take Five : Best Contemporary Tanka, Volume 3.

Poet, editor, anthologist, and festival director, Kala Ramesh has been a foremost advocate and practitioner of haiku and allied Japanese poetry forms in India, including tanka, haibun and renku. Kala's initiatives culminated in founding 'INhaiku' in 2013, to bring Indian haikai poets together. In addition to her own prize-winning writing, she has a prolific record as an editor of collections of haiku and tanka anthologies. Kala was on the editorial board of Take Five: The Best Contemporary Tanka 2009, 2010 and 2011.

M. Kei

the last day of December
a grasshopper
gets off
a green pepper from Chile
and surveys his new home

Previously appeared in Take Five : Best Contemporary Tanka, Volume 3.

M. Kei is a tall ship sailor and award-winning poet who lives on Maryland's Eastern Shore. He is the editor of Atlas Poetica : A Journal of World Tanka, and Stacking Stones, An Anthology of Short Tanka Sequences. His most recent collection of poetry is January, A Tanka Diary. He is also the author of the award-winning gay Age of Sail adventure novels, Pirates of the Narrow Seas (http://www.atlaspoetica.org/buy-novels/). He can be followed on Twitter @kujakupoet, or visit AtlasPoetica.org.

Mel Goldberg

I read menus
in restaurants
hoping
they will tell me
something important

Previously appeared in Take Five : Best Contemporary Tanka, Volume 3.

Mel Goldberg taught literature and writing in California, Illinois, Arizona and as a Fulbright Exchange Teacher Stanground College in Cambridgeshire, England. He took early retirement from teaching and moved to Sedona, Arizona, where he continued to write and taught literature and writing at Yavapai College. Mel and his wife bought a small motor home and traveled throughout the US, Canada, and Mexico for seven years. They chose to settle in the village of Ajijic, in the state of Jalisco, Mexico, where they joined the small ex-pat artist and writing community.

Michael McClintock

the day before
heading off to the Army,
my father and friends
smiling into the camera—
smart, funny, and immortal

Previously appeared in Take Five : Best Contemporary Tanka, Volume 3.

Michael McClintock lives with his wife, fine artist Karen, in the San Joaquin Valley of central California, after a long career in public library administration in Los Angeles. His work as poet, editor and critic of English language tanka and haiku have been foundational to the development and history of both genres.

Paul Smith

the warm spring breeze
has made a hole
in me
and planted
something green

Previously appeared in Take Five : Best Contemporary Tanka, Volume 3.

Paul Smith lives in Worcester England! His passions include old time blues, making cigar box guitars and writing little poems!

Raquel D. Bailey

in the rain
he asks for
one last chance
and I leave him standing
with my answer and the moon

Previously appeared in Take Five : Best Contemporary Tanka, Volume 3.

R. D. Bailey earned her B. A. degree from FSU. Her literary works appear in more than 30 publications worldwide. She is the winner of the 2019 Harold G. Henderson Haiku Awards and the 2019 Tokusen (2nd Prize) Winner, 24th Intl. "KUSAMAKURA" Haiku Competition, Japan. Ms. Bailey is originally from Jamaica.

Roary Williams

she and he
lights at each end
of the house
turning on and off
at different times

Previously appeared in Take Five : Best Contemporary Tanka, Volume 3.

Roary Williams lives with his wife in the middle of nowhere up near a mountain in the high desert of New Mexico. His landlady has several horses and a bunch of dogs he hangs out with sometimes. He tries to live in zen.

Saeko Ogi / 小城　小枝子

Amelia Fielden, Japanese-English translator

アメリア・フィールデン、日英翻訳家

大空に散りし神風歌四首遺せし義兄の声に胸凍る

hearing the voice
of my brother-in-law
in those four tanka he left
before his kamikaze death,
my blood runs cold

Previously appeared in Take Five : Best Contemporary Tanka, Volume 3.

かつて、「Take Five: 現代短歌秀歌五首」の第三集に作品がとられた。

Saeko Ogi is a tanka poet and tanka translator. A member of the Araragi-ha Tanka Group in Japan since 2003. Born in Tokyo, has lived in Canberra nearly for 50 years. Contributing tanka both in Japanese and English to anthologies and collections, being actively involved in tanka activities; translating, presenting talks in symposiums and facilitating a tanka Group in Canberra. Previously appeared in Take Five: Best Contemporary Tanka, Volume 3 and 4.

Amelia Fielden is a professional translator of Japanese literature, and a keen writer of Japanese form poetry in English. Her latest publication is 'These Purple Years', a life in tanka.

Sanford Goldstein

hospitalized again:
I walk this narrow corridor
in the autumn dawn,
and once more the sudden gift
of a stranger's friendly face

Previously appeared in Take Five : Best Contemporary Tanka, Volume 3.

Sanford Goldstein is more than 90 years old. He has been writing tanka for more than fifty years. He continues to live in Japan with his friend Kazuaki Wakui.

IV. Tanka Sequence for Translation:

What the City Whispered To My Grandmother

Kath Abela Wilson

in her small room
far from the river
I watch her
serenely she builds
her own pyramid

always on the watch
at the back window
she prays
for what
will happen next

she lets down her hair
in a net of hail marys
they climb back up
land on the roof
to keep her awake

her blue and pink
canvas of day
feeds the night
always about
to arrive

behind the sheer curtain
alligators
are always waiting
we catch the whispering city
in our mouths

Previously appeared in Take Five : Best Contemporary Tanka, Volume 4.

Kath Abela Wilson is the creator and leader of Poets on Site in Pasadena, Caifornia. She performs her poetry accompanied by her husband, Rick Wilson on flutes of the world. Her two chapbooks The Owl Still Asking and Driftwood Monster, 2017, Moria Press, are available from Lulu. Her new book of free verse Figures of Humor and Strange Beauty, Glass Lyre Press, 2018 is available on Amazon. It concludes with a cherita.

V. Tanka Prose for Translation:

In Living Muscle

Larry Kimmel

A taupe snake, thick as a firehose, and like nothing I've ever seen in Massachusetts, before or since, was ejected from beneath the car ahead of mine. It coiled and leapt some three or more feet above the asphalt. There was no time, no way, to miss its writhing hop. It must have leapt at least two times before it was tumbled, with a blunt thumping noise, beneath my own car, and what I saw in the rearview mirror was anguish sculpted in living muscle.

evening breeze,
a quiver travels the driveway's fringe
of ferns
like a shiver of bad news
along a spine

Previously appeared in Take Five : Best Contemporary Tanka, Volume 2.

Larry Kimmel was born in Johnstown, Pennsylvania. He lives quietly in the hills of western Massachusetts. His most recent books are "shards and dust;" "outer edges;" & "long-stemmed roses."

Review: *Light-Borne Rain* by Shelia Windsor & Larry Kimmel

Reviewed by Patricia Prime

light-borne rain
Shelia Windsor & Larry Kimmel Winifred Press, Colrain, MA, USA. (2019). RRP: $US 5.99. Pb, 115pp.
SBN-13: 978-0-9864328-4-2.

Sheila Windsor and Larry Kimmel's light-borne rain is a collection of cherita. While fitting into the category of poetry, the texts sit somewhere in the hybrid zones of Japanese forms. What I take from the cherita is the indefinable chimera, offered to the poets in terms of making meaning and of exploring their chosen subject matter. It's a kind of experimental poetry where fiction, biography, autobiography and plain speaking meet lyricism. All these points are certainly true of the collection. Windsor and Kimmel's passion for, and interest in, their subjects and the cherita form, is evident throughout their work and, light-borne rain takes this to a new level.

Each of the one hundred verses was written between the 25 July 2016 – 10 September 2016. the verses are published centrally, one per page. Verses by Larry Kimmel are in normal type; those by Sheila Windsor are in italics. Cover art and illustrations are by Sheila Windsor.

Here is a poetry firmly rooted in the present tense, alive with verbs. Often, the events happen to the poets in a first-hand account, as in the following cherita (2):

a church in Rouen

we teeter towards
the tipping point

your skin, mine,
as dusty webs
intone unfinished psalms

It is a relational poetry, full of "I", "my", "her" and "we". Though often light-hearted and informal in language and style, the cherita are amazingly deft and clever, as in this one on page 15:

a coffee bean

whose long odyssey from
Columbian field
to Boston coffee cup

blossoms on my tongue
a tanka

I enjoyed the personal approach and fragments of lyricism. The cherita range in subject matter from Kimmel's "ventriloquist's dummy" to Windsor's "seashell". There's enough psychology in the subjects to spark every reader's interest. The "silver eagle" is opposed with "the sparrow"; "a wintry strand" is partnered with "snowflakes"; "cruel laughter" is contrasted by "a shriek of merriment". The interweaving of language and personal experience is a feature of the collection, as we see in the following cherita: the first by Kimmel and the second by Windsor:

all those jukebox dimes—

to ride the crest of the wave
to be the voice of an era

a pack of Camels, a Pabst
& Ray Charles, all for a buck
back in the day

*

time for home

beachcomber and boat
of cobbled things

were always
going to go
their separate ways

There are many ways into these poems. Their imagery is often surreal but also strongly sensual. They often cast a romantic and nostalgic eye over childhood, home and ageing, love and desire. In the following cherita, Kimmel reminisces about a chill October evening, and the Jack Daniels and tools left behind presumably by his father (85):

October

I fill the wood bin
take the chill off evening—

Jack Daniels on the shelf,
half-full—his tools
the way he left them

While the following cherita by Windsor also reminisces about the past, it is a poem of happiness and joy to be in the garden, where a couple think about the flowers that will grow in the future (90):

a thousand smiles

where the
sweet peas were

pods of fragrant
pastel tomorrows . . . more
than you and I will know

In some sense, all the cherita could be regarded as letters to the wider world, arranged by specific moments. Here are two extremely talented poets capturing moments of poetry, with sensual, personal, and observational cherita. This is a book for readers who like a variety of subject matter, who like to dip into a book at odd moments or who wish to devour the whole collection in one sitting. It's the kind of poetry we can enjoy over and over again.

ANNOUNCEMENTS

Atlas Poetica will publish short announcements in any language up to 300 words in length on a space-available basis. Announcements may be edited for brevity, clarity, grammar, or any other reason. Send announcements in the body of an email to: AtlasPoetica@gmail.com — do not send attachments.

it's a secret place *edition 3:12 of the cherita*, Published

This edition of it's a secret place showcases 90 fine cherita and cherita terbalik from writers and poets who hail from UK, USA, Singapore, New Zealand/ Australia/ Canada/ India/ Poland/ Romania and Ireland.

http://www.thecherita.com/itsasecretplace/

it's a secret place is the twelfth and last edition for our third year. the cherita begins its fourth year next month in June 2020 with its 23rd birthday on the 22 June 2020.

There's still no let-up on our Covid-19 lockdown in the UK. Buying food and essentials now require queueing with social distancing being de rigueur. A once ordinary routine has become time consuming but I thank my lucky stars that I am still able to perform this weekly trip unlike the huge numbers of people stricken by this unrelenting virus, and being kept away from their loved ones. The uncertainty of ever meeting up again with their family looms large over all these patients. My nights are full of whispered prayers for all the sick and dying.

I urge you to find your very own secret place during this testing time – I call mine my spiritual oasis where I find myself armchair travelling to become the wandering storyteller of my dreams. Writing short form poetry has always been a panacea for healing for me, and helped me through the tougher times in my life. These minimal words can take one to a place of wonder and light when our illusory world grows darker with the unresolved problems of a day.

Since Friday 10 April, I have been posting published cherita from the cherita daily on our *Lockdown Cherita*, a new feature on our website

http://www.thecherita.com/announcements/

My hope is that these special cherita will not only help inspire all aspiring Cherita poets and writers to start telling their own stories in 6 lines but also inspire and spur on our established cherita poets and writers to lift and write us all out of this lockdown period with more of their timeless cherita.

Please be aware that for the next 5 days, there will be no *lockdown cherita* whilst the edition announcement for #3:12 is up. *Lockdown Cherita* will resume with its eighteenth cherita on Wednesday 6 May.

I have edited and still as I have all the other editions of the cherita, to be experienced two ways. It can be read as one storybook but also as an anthology of individual poems. Two reading experiences within one book, filled with stories of Life, Love and Loss.

cherita terbalik continues to capture the imagination of poets and there are again fine examples in this edition.

Featured Poets as they appear in it's a secret place:

ai li/ Luis Cuauhtemoc Berriozabal/ Taura Scott/ Kath Abela Wilson/ Larry Kimmel/ Joanna Ashwell/ Patricia Prime/ Carol Purington/ Myrto E. Angeloglou/ Keitha Keyes/ Peter Jastermsky/ Jackie Chou/ Ruth Kay/ Cynthia Anderson/ Tim Gardiner/ Debbie Strange/ Vicki Moreno/ Tiffany Shaw-Diaz/ Mekhled Alzaza/ Grace Galton/ Robert Horrobin/ Gregory Longenecker/ Neelam Dadhwal/ Paweł Markiewicz/ S.Radhamani/ Réka Nyitrai/ Ron Scully/ paula song sarmonpal/ Partha Sarkar/ Elva Lauter/ Jonathan Vos Post/ James Haddad/ Isabella Kramer/ Maryalicia Post/ Tim Callahan/

EXAMPLE OF WORK from it's a secret place:

in maple shade

hand upon
the latch I turn

to look at where
the sky and earth
meet

Larry Kimmel

The cherita lighthouse has been awarded to the following writers and poets in this edition for their timeless Cherita :

Larry Kimmel/ Peter Jastermsky/ Jackie Chou/ Kath Abela Wilson/ Joanna Ashwell/ Debbie Strange/ Vicki Moreno/ Tiffany Shaw-Diaz/ Mekhled Alzaza/ paula song sarmonpal/

I have enjoyed the challenge of selecting and collating for this edition of the cherita and hope that you will find the cherita within worthy of a campfire gathering and the sharing of meaningful stories.

If this new edition strikes a chord with you, please feel free to review, comment on Amazon or give feedback directly to me. Many thanks.
ai li
editor, www.thecherita.com

Announcing *light-borne rain (a two-voice improvisation)* by Larry Kimmel and sheila windsor

If a lot of poetry comes across as studied and overworked, then *light-borne rain*, the new book of collaborative cherita by Larry Kimmel and Sheila Windsor will be a welcome relief. Allowing themselves no longer than 30 minutes to craft a response to the other's piece, Larry and Sheila are at their buoyant best. These cherita exude wit and playfulness, as the poets' use of an eclectic assortment of images make the results feel effortless. This is a book I'll dip into frequently to savor the craft, as well as the partnership, between these two fine poets. —Peter Jastermsky

Sheila Windsor and Larry Kimmel's *light-borne rain* is an engaging cherita conversation between two accomplished writers who have mastered the art of juxtaposing their work. Readers will be entertained by this "jam session", which features eclectic topics ranging from Pabst to Pinot Noir, Gregorian chant to Dylan, Sappho to Rimbaud, Monet to Dali, Pooh to Barbie, and everything in between! —Debbie Strange

Examples of the Work

betrayed

a sea of ghostly thumbnails
laughing . . . laughing . . .

toward what grotesque end
this outré twist
of fate

Larry Kimmel

a church in Rouen

we teeter towards
the tipping point

your skin, mine,
as dusty webs
intone unfinished psalms

sheila windsor

Order Here: http://www.winfredpress.com/blog

Drifting Sands Haibun & Tanka Prose Journal Call for Submissions

Announcing the launch of a new online journal for promoting English-language haibun and tanka prose poetry. *Drifting Sands Online Journal* is a volunteer project designed to bring poets together with readers.

"Haibun and its cousin Tanka Prose contemplate the gamut of human experience. They are rich with observations and have the potential to impact lives. drifting-sands-haibun's goal is to propagate these important literary forms by providing a platform for publishing poets' works and expanding readership." says Richard Grahn, founder of drifting-sands-haibun. "The journal is a new grain of sand on an old beach ready for a poet to pick it up and pack it into a sand-castle."

Features and benefits of drifting-sands-haibun include:

– Open to all English-language haibun and tanka prose poets.
– Simultaneous submissions and previously-published poems welcome.
– No-fee submissions.

https://drifting-sands-haibun.org is online now and accepting submissions for the first issue. For more information, please visit our submissions page at https://drifting-sands-haibun.org/submissions.
Richard Grahn, Editor

Velocities and Drifts of Wind

Velocities and Drifts of Winds by Geoffrey Winch (ISBN: 978-1-913329-15-0) is due for publication in September 2020 by Dempsey and Windle Publishing www.dempseyandwindle.com. Seventy poems including haiku, tanka, cherita, haibun, tanka prose, tanka sequences and vers libre, it is themed around the winds of change—past, present and personal.

Educational Use Notice

Keibooks of Perryville, Maryland, USA, publisher of the journal, *Atlas Poetica : A Journal of World Tanka*, is dedicated to tanka education in schools and colleges, at every level. It is our intention and our policy to facilitate the use of *Atlas Poetica* and related materials to the maximum extent feasible by educators at every level of school and university studies.

Educators, without individually seeking permission from the publisher, may use *Atlas Poetica : A Journal of World Tanka*'s online digital editions and print editions as primary or ancillary teaching resources. Copyright law 'Fair Use' guidelines and doctrine should be interpreted very liberally with respect to *Atlas Poetica* precisely on the basis of our explicitly stated intention herein. This statement may be cited as an effective permission to use *Atlas Poetica* as a text or resource for studies. Proper attribution of any excerpt to *Atlas Poetica* is required. This statement applies equally to digital resources and print copies of the journal.

Individual copyrights of poets, authors, artists, etc., published in *Atlas Poetica* are their own property and are not meant to be compromised in any way by the journal's liberal policy on 'Fair Use.' Any educator seeking clarification of our policy for a particular use may email the Editor of *Atlas Poetica* at AtlasPoetica@gmail.com. We welcome innovative uses of our resources for tanka education.

Atlas Poetica
Keibooks
P O Box 346
Perryville, MD 21903
AtlasPoetica.org

Editorial Biographies

M. Kei is the editor of *Atlas Poetica* and was the editor-in-chief of *Take Five : Best Contemporary Tanka*. His most recent project is *Stacking Stones, An Anthology of Short Tanka Sequences*. He is a tall ship sailor in real life and has published nautical novels featuring a gay protagonist, *Pirates of the Narrow Seas*. His most recent poetry collection is *January, A Tanka Diary*.

Grunge is an Indo-American member of the LGBT community who specializes in urban tanka. He is currently the editorial assistant for Keibooks, and lives in South Florida with a collection of pet arthropods, an ancient cat, and a pudgy leopard gecko.

Kira Nash lives in France for the second time and hopes that she'll soon be able to root herself. She finds joy in cups of tea with her husband and cuddles with her cat; she loves gardening and being in the water. The human world bewilders her, but flowers, starlight, and sunshine sing her soul to peace. Kira works as a writer, editor, artist, and teacher, and can be found at www.kiakari.com.

Our 'butterfly' is actually an Atlas moth (*Attacus atlas*), the largest butterfly / moth in the world. It comes from the tropical regions of Asia. Image from the 1921 *Les insectes agricoles d'époque*.

Publications by Keibooks

Anthologies

Stacking Stones : Short Tanka Sequences

Neon Graffiti : Tanka of Urban Life

Bright Stars, An Organic Tanka Anthology (Vols. 1 – 7)

Take Five : Best Contemporary Tanka (Vol. 4)

Fire Pearls (Vols. 1 – 2) : Short Masterpieces of the Heart

Journals

Atlas Poetica : A Journal of World Tanka

M. Kei's Poetry Collections

January, A Tanka Diary

Slow Motion : The Log of a Chesapeake Bay Skipjack
tanka and short forms

Heron Sea : Short Poems of the Chesapeake Bay
tanka and short forms

M. Kei's Novels

Pirates of the Narrow Seas 1 : The Sallee Rovers
Pirates of the Narrow Seas 2 : Men of Honor
Pirates of the Narrow Seas 3 : Iron Men
Pirates of the Narrow Seas 4 : Heart of Oak

Man in the Crescent Moon : A Pirates of the Narrow Seas Adventure
The Sea Leopard : A Pirates of the Narrow Seas Adventure

Fire Dragon

Tanka Collections

Three-Part Harmony, by Debbie Strange

Warp and Weft, Tanka Threads, by Debbie Strange

Black Genji and Other Contemporary Tanka, by Matsukaze

October Blues and Other Contemporary Tanka, by Matsukaze

flowers to the torch : American Tanka Prose, by peter fiore

Tanka by Joy McCall

this is my song, by Joy McCall
side by side, with Larry Kimmel
on the cusp encore, a year of tanka, by Joy McCall
fieldgates, tanka sequences, by Joy McCall
on the cusp, a year of tanka, by Joy McCall
rising mist, fieldstones, by Joy McCall
hedgerows, tanka pentaptychs, by Joy McCall
circling smoke, scattered bones, by Joy McCall

Tanka by Sanford Goldstein

Tanka Left Behind 1968 : Tanka from the Notebooks of Sanford Goldstein, by Sanford Goldstein
Tanka Left Behind : Tanka from the Notebooks of Sanford Goldstein, by Sanford Goldstein
This Short Life, Minimalist Tanka, by Sanford Goldstein

Made in the USA
Monee, IL
23 June 2020